Tackling Marriage

Football Lessons on Being a Godly Husband

Jerrod Nelson

WESTBOW°
PRESS
A DIVISION OF THOMAS NELSON
& ZONDERVAN

Scripture quotations are from The Holy Bible, English Standard Version® (ESV®), copyright © 2001 by Crossway, a publishing ministry of Good News Publishers. Used by permission. All rights reserved.

WestBow Press books may be ordered through booksellers or by contacting:

WestBow Press
A Division of Thomas Nelson & Zondervan
1663 Liberty Drive
Bloomington, IN 47403
www.westbowpress.com
1 (866) 928-1240

ISBN: 978-1-4908-8823-1 (sc)
ISBN: 978-1-4908-8825-5 (hc)
ISBN: 978-1-4908-8824-8 (e)

Print information available on the last page.

WestBow Press rev. date: 08/03/2015

To Lindsey,

who plays the most important position in my life

Acknowledgements

Thanks to Justin, Tom, Chad, Casey, and Darren,
who were there when this idea first started.
Thanks to Dave, John, and Brian, who read
the book and gave me great advice.
Special thanks to Pastor Chad, who read the book in detail.
Thanks to Cross Books for the opportunity.
Thanks to ESPN, Sports Illustrated, and football-reference.com
for historical and statistical information.

Contents

Introduction

When my brother-in-law, Justin, was getting married in the summer of 2010, he asked me to be his Best Man. I gladly accepted and got to work doing all of the things that a Best Man is supposed to do before the wedding, which it turns out is very little. On the wedding day I ended up doing a lot, but before then the only real responsibility I had was planning his bachelor party. So I set up a weekend at a cabin in Northern Minnesota where we played lawn games, grilled steaks and burgers (and Spam, believe it or not), played a round of golf, and swam in the creek. On one of the evenings we were there, Justin had asked me to do a sort of devotional for the group. That's where the idea for this book was born.

Justin is a big football fan, and actually played and coached the offensive line at the University of St. Thomas in Minnesota, so I thought that maybe I could connect marriage to football somehow. Then I started thinking about all of the different positions and roles on a team and how we fill a lot of those same types of roles for our wives. I got to work making the connections and picking out some Bible verses for each one, and the result was something that was focused on the Lord and His plan for marriage, but still interesting and fun for a bunch of guys who are sports fans.

And that's where I hope this book finds you. Interesting and fun and related to something you enjoy, but still focused on God's Word and the serious task he has given us as husbands. And if you're not into football or sports at all, I hope you can still learn something from this book, and that it makes you consider the ways you love your wife. I'm not saying that I'm perfect in all of these areas or that I have it all figured out, far from it. But maybe it opens a discussion about how we can all glorify God as men, and that's really the end goal.

One important thing to remember is that none of the analogies with the positions are perfect. We've all seen coaches and players who scream and curse and intimidate, are selfish and distracting, indulge in poor behavior on and off the field, and really are just nothing we want to be for our wives. But there are coaches and players who are respectful, joyful, make good choices, and are good examples of how a man can honor God. But remember, those men are still sinful and make mistakes. The football analogy can help us think about our roles and responsibilities as Godly husbands, but our ultimate example is Jesus Christ, and in the end we want our marriage to look like more than a football team, we want it to look like Christ and His church (Ephesians 5:23-24, 32, English Standard Version).

With that in mind, I hope you enjoy this book, and that it challenges you to become more like Christ and to love your wife and fill your roles as a husband in a God-honoring, loving way.

As Your Wife's Scout...
You Need to be Her Student.

Any football team will tell you that before any practices take place, before any game is played, before any plan is executed, and before any win is celebrated or loss grieved, there has to be careful study done of a lot of things that will help the team be successful. That responsibility falls to the team's scouts. Instead of getting on the field and banging heads, yelling at referees, or scoring touchdowns, the scouts watch, study, and document everything they notice about other teams and players. This information is incredibly valuable to a team so they can know ahead of time what works or doesn't work against another team, how another player responds to certain strategies, what the other team will do in certain situations, and all kinds of other things. Obtaining information is key to success, and the best way to do that is close study. Men, as your wife's husband, you need to be her scout.

History is a little fuzzy, but it seems like the first scout to watch upcoming opponents to help his team was Fido Murphy, who worked for the Steelers and the Bears in the early 1940's. He is considered one of the smartest men to ever work in professional football and had an impact on just about every facet of the game, not the least of which was the way that teams scouted opponents and prepared game plans. Then, in 1946, the owner of the Los Angeles Rams, Dan Reeves, hired Eddie Kotal as the first man who really studied and scouted college players. At that time most teams would find college talent based only on magazine or newspaper articles and press releases from the colleges. Kotal was sent to actually watch the players play and practice and evaluate them so the Rams would know whom to get. The plan worked as the Rams played in the league championship in 1949, 1950, and 1951, which was the year they finally won it. They played in another championship game in 1955, and from 1949-1956 the Rams had a record of 60-33-3. Through the 50's, other teams picked up on this strategy and scouting became one of the most important aspects of a team's success. Now, every team has a full scouting department, and every spring the NFL runs the Scouting Combine where college prospects can show their skills in front of scouts for every pro team. In addition, every team will travel to watch certain players, or bring in players for private workouts. Outside companies have even set up scouting services for colleges and professional teams to use, and online scouting rankings are extremely popular as the college National Signing Day and the NFL Draft approach. Advance scouting has also come a long way. Not only do scouts go and watch upcoming opponents, but they pore over videos, stat sheets, historical tendencies, and anything else they think will give them an edge to win.

It makes sense, really. If you want to be as successful at something as you possibly can, find out as much about it as you possibly can. I teach high school English, and it took me five years of college to become a teacher. Then it took me about another five years to become a good teacher. During that time, I read fiction and nonfiction, books about education and classroom management, articles about assessing writing and best practice, novels for adolescents and pre-adolescents, and all kinds of other things. I wanted to be good at my job, so I studied. That philosophy seems pretty common. No matter what you do, if you want to be good at it, you have to study. And it's not just limited to careers. I've seen guys put more study into their yearly fantasy football draft than anything else they encounter, and those guys usually do really well at the game. They've decided that fantasy football is important enough to warrant that much time and energy, so they study it. Whether that's a good use of your time and energy is debatable, but the point remains that close study is really important to being good at something.

Unfortunately, we apply that principle to our jobs, our hobbies, and even our games, but rarely do men apply it to the most important job they have: being a husband. It's one of the greatest callings that God has given to us, and yet most men seem to think that they'll just figure it out as they go along. But that way of thinking doesn't seem to apply to anything else we do, just marriage. We'll spend hours and hours learning and studying how to be better in so many other areas of our lives, while our task of being a husband is shoved aside in favor of other pursuits. But if you think you're just going to "figure it out" and somehow magically become a great husband, you're in for a disappointment, and so is your wife. Just like anything else, and even more than most things, being a Godly, Biblical, good husband requires study and learning. You will not just wake up one day to find that you are an excellent husband who lives out all of God's principles. Rather, if you don't study it, you will wake up to discover that a lot of time has gone by that you can't get back. I can't say it any more plainly than this:

Just like anything else, if you want to be a Godly husband, you won't just know how to do it, you have to learn how to do it.

One of the most well-known verses in the Bible illustrates this point nicely, Proverbs 3:5, which says, "Trust in the Lord with all your heart, and do not lean on your own understanding." Our own understanding and knowledge is insufficient; we must follow the teaching of the Lord. Those who think that they know enough already and can't be bothered to learn more or study at all are spoken of in Proverbs 1:7, "The fear of the Lord is the beginning of knowledge; fools despise wisdom and instruction." The Bible makes it plain. If you believe that you have it all figured out and are doing a fine job with no room for growth, you are a fool. It's when we acknowledge that we don't know everything and still need to grow that real learning can happen. It's also important to understand that your path to knowledge will take a while, you won't just get everything overnight. Paul makes a nice analogy to the church in 1 Corinthians when he says, "But I, brothers, could not address you as spiritual people, but as people of the flesh, as infants in Christ. I fed you with milk, not solid food, for you were not ready for it. And even now you are not yet ready" (3:1-2). If you're just starting to study, start with realistic goals and ideas. Like Paul says, we don't feed babies steaks, they can only drink milk. As an infant in Christ, you must start with that "milk" and work your way up to a juicy porterhouse, and that's okay. Don't compare your own learning to anyone else, just make sure that you are learning and growing and seeking God's will. It's when the growth stops happening that it becomes a problem. If we start studying and get the big ideas but then never move past that, we're like a ten-year-old who is still only drinking milk and doesn't eat any solid foods. At some point, to keep growing, you have to challenge yourself and get into something new.

So the obvious question is, where does that learning come from? What should we study? The first thing that we should study is the Bible itself, and not only the passages that concern husbands and marriage. The Bible is not a book of fables, as some would have you believe, it is a book that serves to guide us, teach us, and lead us in the way that the Lord would have us go, and it is useful for us in every aspect of life. Paul wrote in 2 Timothy 3:16-17 that "All Scripture is breathed out by God and profitable for teaching, for reproof, for correction, and for training in righteousness, that the man of God may be complete, equipped for every good work." It's not just certain passages that we need to study, or single verses in a vacuum, but the entire Bible. *All scripture* helps us learn, grow, and live the way God wants us to live. So it's not a matter of just picking out the verses that talk about being a husband and trying to apply those, it's a matter of using the entire Bible to learn and grow in every area of your life, which will in turn help you become an even better husband. The Bible tells us that if we study it and live it that we will be blessed in many ways. Romans 15:4 says, "For whatever was written in former days was written for our instruction, that through endurance and through the encouragement of the Scriptures we might have hope." If we hold fast to the Bible and use it for our own study and learning, we will be encouraged and have hope beyond anything else we ask for. Joshua 1:8 makes it even more plain, saying, "This Book of the Law shall not depart from your mouth, but you shall meditate on it day and night, so that you may be careful to do according to all that is written in it. For then you will make your way prosperous, and then you will have good success." Meditating on something "day and night" does not sound like two minutes spent on one verse before rushing off to work or school. It sounds like careful, close, continual study, and with that comes success. What that success looks like will be up to God. It may include success with your family, at your job, financially, or many other things, but ultimately the success we gain from studying God's Word is that we are able to be in relationship with Him and can try to be as much like Christ as we possibly can. Without that, no other success is worth having and we will not be able to someday be with Him in Heaven.

Jesus even went so far as to say, "If you abide in my word, you are truly my disciples" (John 8:31), implying that those who do not spend time studying the Bible are not disciples of Jesus at all. That is not an idea that should be taken lightly, but it makes sense. If a scout was to give his team a report on an upcoming opponent or college player without having seen them play or looking at any pictures or film, what would his team say? They would probably wonder how he got any information at all, and he probably wouldn't be working for the team for much longer if he didn't change his habits. What will God say if we stand before Him and tell Him that we didn't read the Bible much or think about what it said? He will not tell us that it was okay, we don't need to read the Bible to follow Him. It would not go well and we would not have "good success." But studying the Bible doesn't just benefit us, our study of the Bible also benefits our wives.

If we study and learn what the Bible teaches, we will be able to teach and lead our families in the ways of the Lord. Everyone needs someone to help guide them in their understanding and study of the Bible, and we should be our wives' first option. When she has a question, or is wondering about something she heard or read, or is looking for verses and passages on a particular topic, her husband should be the first stop she makes for help. If he isn't, she'll either remain clueless or, worse, go to someone else for guidance. If that other person is a man, she then has reason to respect him more than her own husband. Of course, there are men who are there to help us, like our pastors and elders, but if our wives get help from them it should be in the context of the marriage relationship as well. When my wife had a question that I didn't know the answer to on a pretty big topic, we went to talk to our pastor together. That way, we both learned and grew in our knowledge. It was okay that I didn't know the answer because I was willing to learn with her, grow with her, and help her understand the things we learn. How would she have felt if I had told her, "I don't know, go ask the pastor, he probably knows" and left it at that? How can she respect someone who doesn't learn, doesn't grow, and doesn't help her understand? You don't always have to have the answer immediately; there will be plenty of times when you don't. But since you have already established a willingness to study the Word, you will be able to study the issue or question she has brought to you, either on your own or together, and find an answer that will help her. It is your job to learn and shepherd your family so that you can feed them spiritually.

One well-known marriage passage is Ephesians 5. In it, Paul writes that a husband should "sanctify her [his wife], having cleansed her by the washing of water with the word" (v. 26). We'll discuss this passage more in the Quarterback chapter, but the main point here is that it is our job as husbands to bring the Word of God to our wives so that they can learn and grow in Christ as well. It's not enough for a man to grow and learn by himself, he must help his wife do it too.

Another benefit to the close study of the Bible is that when your wife brings you an idea or a plan for the marriage or the family, you will be able to respond appropriately. If you have already studied the issue, you can either humbly agree or disagree with her and explain Biblically why you are doing so. If you have not yet studied the issue, you can take some time to do that, seeking what God says about it, and then return to her with the proper reaction. Imagine if a coach came up with a game plan and then asked his scout if it would work, only to hear the scout say, "I don't know, I haven't looked at the film and I don't have time right now, so just do whatever you think is best and hopefully it works." The coach would feel like he was just blindly trying something without any guidance or confidence that it may work, the same way a wife will feel if she wants to try something and is dismissed by her husband with no thought or discussion. If she then tries it and fails, bitter feelings can develop because she was not given any help. But when the husband studies and helps his wife, even if the thing fails, they can know that they tried it together, looked to God's word for guidance, and can now figure out why it failed and either change the way they're doing it or abandon it completely. When our oldest child was three years old and our second child was not even two, my wife came to me with the idea of homeschooling the kids when the time came. I very calmly asked her if she was crazy and where such a ridiculous idea came from, and I explained that as a public school teacher, I could not very well homeschool my own kids. After a short time and talking with her about it, I realized that reaction was not helpful and was even disrespectful of her and her ideas. I also thought about where I was getting my opinion from. It was only from my own stereotypes of homeschool children and families, as well as my fear of how it would look to my colleagues. Realizing that, I decided to study what the Bible said about the issue, and looked to other books about raising children as well as the multiple other families in our church who homeschooled. After studying all of those things and having a lot of conversations with my wife, I decided that she was right all along and that homeschooling was the best decision for our family. As I write this, our oldest is about to start kindergarten at home and I couldn't be more excited about it. If I had not looked to the Word and studied what God said about the education of children and the role of parents like us, I would have missed a great opportunity to help my kids and my wife make the best decision for their futures. After making that initial decision, we continued to study and read and talk to other families about what curriculum to use, how to set up a schedule, how to organize the house, and all kinds of other things that will hopefully help us be successful.

This is a good time to mention that nobody else's study can be taken and used as your own. I studied and decided to homeschool my children. That was for my family, not for yours. You don't get to take a decision I made and copy it while saying, "Well, he studied it Biblically, so I'll just do what he did." You need to study for your own family in your own situation. You may be guided in your study by other people, and you may even end up making the same decision they did, but it's because you learned about the topic and made the best decision for your family, not just because you're copying what someone else did.

Notice that while studying starts and ends with the Bible, it doesn't just stay there the whole time. We always need to stay focused on the Bible, but other ways of gaining knowledge and guidance can be helpful as well. There are parts of the Bible that can be difficult to understand, and there's a lot of misinformation out there, so using books that can help you, sermons from other pastors, and especially other people you know to guide you can be a very important part of the studying process. Again, all of those other resources should be focused on and use the Bible as their main source, but it's okay to admit that you need some help understanding, or some guidance about where to find certain topics in the Bible, or things like that. The more you learn, the more you'll be able to help other people later, first your wife and then maybe other men who are seeking guidance as well. Just remember when you're using those outside resources to hold it up against the Bible and make sure that they are saying the same thing.

After studying the Bible as a whole, the next important things to study are the roles that you fill in your life. We are all a creation of God, and after that every man is a son, and the vast majority of men will become a husband and a father. Knowing how God wants us to perform those roles is vital to being successful in them. Like I said earlier, you won't just wake up the morning after you get married and know how to be a good husband. You'll have to spend time studying and figuring it out. The bad part is that most men think that learning how to be a husband begins when they get married, but it starts much earlier than that. As a child and a teenager, you study the people around you, most obviously your parents. If you can recognize the good and bad things that other married couples do as you grow up, you will already be learning how a Godly marriage functions. As you get older and you have a more serious relationship, the studying continues. Read what the Bible says about being a husband even before you're married, and talk to your father or other married men you trust and respect. Listen to sermons on the topics of marriage, sex, and family. All of those things will give you a head start on being a good husband before you ever get married, and it's never too early to start studying. Even if marriage doesn't seem like it's in your near future, it probably will be someday, and the longer you study something, the more you'll know about it and be able to put it into practice when the time comes. Conversely, if you're already married, it's never too late to start studying either. If it feels like you haven't been a good husband up to this point, whether for one month or fifty years, you can make a decision to begin today to start studying how God wants you to live, for Him and for your wife. Of course, it will be different than the unmarried man because you'll be learning on the job, but in some ways that will make it easier because you'll be able to see all of the principles you're learning unfold in your own marriage and experience the difference that a Godly marriage can make.

After being a student of the Bible and a student of your roles, the next step is to become a student of your wife. Where does she come from? What does she like? How does she react to things? What are her strengths and weaknesses? What makes her feel loved? Knowing as much as you can about her will help you be a better husband because you will know what she needs from you. You'll know when to push her and when to hold back, what she likes as gifts, what's important to her, and a ton of other things that will make her feel like you care about her and appreciate her and actually pay attention to her. Just remember that what you learn may change over time, so you have to be constantly studying her and learning about her. My wife loves to cook, so I bought her kitchen stuff for almost every gift-giving occasion for about five years. It was so easy! I knew she loved to cook, and there is a store at the mall filled with kitchen stuff, so I would go there and pick out something new for her. She appreciated each gift, but I have to think that eventually she got a little tired of it. Finally, one winter, I decided that I would not buy her anything for the kitchen for Christmas. So I started paying attention to other things she might like. I listened to her, watched her reactions, and made note of things that may be good gifts. I ended up getting her a CD from a band she had recently discovered and liked, and a two-person card game because she likes doing activities like that. It took a little extra work, but I could tell she was happy that I had taken the time to figure out what she would want as a gift instead of going to the kitchen store again. When a football scout works hard and studies everything he can to help his team win, they know that he takes his job seriously and they will trust him in the future. When a husband works hard and studies his wife, she knows that he wants to be successful and will trust him as well.

The last point to make on this topic is that the studying and learning never end. Does a football scout use film of the opponent's games from five years ago? Of course not, they get new film and look at it with a fresh perspective. They can take what they know about certain teams or coaches, but they have to combine that with the latest knowledge they've gained to provide an accurate picture that will help the team win. That was my problem with the kitchen gifts. I came up with what I thought was a good way of doing things, but five years later I was still doing it and it wasn't nearly as successful anymore. We fall into that trap with our study of the Bible and our roles too. We may learn a lot from our study, but that doesn't mean the study is over. Just because you've studied something multiple times doesn't mean that you can't learn something new from it. Try looking at it from a different perspective or hearing what someone else thinks about it. But don't ever think that you've learned everything you can. Football scouts will always try to discover something they missed the first time or that they can help their team be better at, and we can always try to grow in our knowledge of the Lord and how he wants us to live as husbands.

As Your Wife's Head Coach... You Need to be Her Planner.

Where does the team start and end? Who gets the credit when things go well, or the blame when things go poorly? Where does the buck stop? The head coach. The head coach is the one who makes decisions, the one who has to get the most out of his players, and, perhaps most importantly, the one who is responsible for planning for the game. Sure, he has assistant coaches and people like that, but ultimately the head coach is held responsible for having his team ready when the game starts.

One of the most vital skills that many people misdirect is that of being properly prepared. Interestingly, we do try to prepare ourselves for certain things. If I'm going somewhere I've never been, I look at a map to figure out where it is and how to get there, otherwise I may get lost. As a high school teacher, when my principal would observe my classroom, I would make sure in the days leading up that everything was ready so nothing would go wrong. My dad spends months planning and re-planning road trips to various baseball stadiums around the country. In fact, he usually has more fun planning the trips than he does actually going on them. So the skill of preparation is not something that is lacking, just something that often gets focused incorrectly.

So if we have this skill, why do we use it in ways that are fun or useful or even important in a basic way, but neglect it in the most important aspects of our lives? I think the answer is two-fold. First, our priorities are messed up, because our hearts are not naturally focused on God, but on ourselves. Sure, we'll look up directions or figure out how we're going to get the new couch through the door before actually trying, but when it comes to our Godly relationships, we are woefully unprepared. Second, a lot of people don't even realize that there are ways to prepare, or even that they need to be prepared in the first place. But proper preparation is absolutely vital to success in any area, whether it be travelling, working, or marriage. Without proper preparation, the task will quickly fall to pieces.

No football coach would go into a game without a game plan. When gameday arrives, the coach has a specific plan in place. And how did he arrive at that plan? Was it just an arbitrary decision or did he throw something together the night before? Of course not. He spends days or even weeks looking at film of his own team and his opponent. He looks at statistics, scouting reports, and even weather forecasts. He picks out his opponent's strengths and weaknesses while at the same time recognizing his own team's strengths and weaknesses. He meticulously plans his course of action so that it will result in the greatest possible success. Men, as your wife's head coach, you need to be her planner.

They need someone who is committed to preparing as much as possible so that success can be pursued with confidence. Would a football team respect a coach who showed up on game day with no plan to win the game? Not at all! They want to see their coach take his role seriously, and to spend his time crafting a game plan so that they can win. What plays are they going to run? How are they going to stop the opponent's best player? What if someone gets hurt, what would they do? The players want to know that the coach has a plan in place that is designed for them to succeed. By the same token, if a woman is going to marry a man, do you think she's encouraged by a guy whose most common answer is "I don't know"? Of course not! She wants to know that he has a plan. Where are they going to live? How will they pay for things? How will they move forward in their life? A woman does not want to hear a guy say, "Well, let's just get married and then we'll probably figure it out." She wants to have confidence in her new husband that he knows how he is going to take care of her and be a good husband for her.

Why should we plan and prepare? Why this emphasis on thinking about the future? Because the Bible exhorts us to make plans and figure out how we can be successful in our relationship with God and others. God planned and prepared the world for thousands of years before sending Jesus for our salvation. Even Jesus himself prepared for about 30 years before starting his ministry here on Earth. And God tells us in His Word that planning and preparation are essential to success. Not success of Earthly things, like money or a nice house or a great job, though He may bless us with those things if He chooses, but success in our relationship with Him and others. Proverbs 14:8 tells us, "The wisdom of the prudent is to discern his way, but the folly of fools is deceiving." How else can you discern God's way besides planning and preparing by reading the Bible, praying, and being a part of a community of believers? Not only are these the tools that He has given us so that we can learn and prepare as our life goes on, they are the means of grace that He has revealed to us. We don't deserve to have those tools, but by His grace he has given them to us so that we can prepare and plan for our lives. And if we do plan in the way that God intends, we will not be disappointed. Later, in Proverbs 21:5, it says, "The plans of the diligent lead surely to abundance, but everyone who is hasty comes only to poverty." The Bible does not offer false hope or fleeting possibility, but says that if we plan properly that we will have success. Paul tells us something similar in 2 Corinthians 9:6 when he says, "whoever sows sparingly will also reap sparingly, and whoever sows bountifully will also reap bountifully." The lesson couldn't be more clear: If you put in the work ahead of time and continue planning for what comes next, you will be rewarded.

Of course, this doesn't mean that you have to have every aspect of every day of your life planned out for the next 30 years. That's unrealistic and impossible. But it does mean that you should have some big things figured out and at least some ideas about how you are going to make your marriage work. Some people may wonder, "Marriage is such a personal thing, there's really no way to understand it until you're in it, right? So how can you prepare for something like that?" It's true, marriage can be difficult, and your wedding is not an end point, you will be learning for the rest of your life. But just because you can't know everything before you get married doesn't mean you shouldn't know anything. So what can you do? Read books about marriage or books specifically written for husbands and wives. Find men who seem to be doing well in their marriage and talk to them about it. Find out what they do, and what works and what doesn't. Listen to sermons, go to conferences, or do any number of things that are available to help you prepare for getting married. But above all, two things are most important when preparing for marriage.

First, talk to your future wife about it. It's important to plan and prepare, but you can't do it in a vacuum. Tell her about what you're learning, discuss the ideas and revelations you've had, ask her opinion about what she wants from you and how she envisions your future. That way, the preparation is being done by both of you. It would be a terrible feeling to plan and prepare for your future only to discover that your new wife thought you would be going in a different direction. It's not your job to make unilateral decisions and drag her along for the ride, it's your job to come up with a plan that is the best for your whole family, and her ideas are a part of that. Our role as husbands is not to be a dictator, but a servant leader.

The other most important aspect of planning for marriage is to study what God says about it. After all, He created it, and in his grace He gives us a lot of guidance concerning how to carry it out in a way that honors and glorifies Him and brings it to His ultimate purpose of making it a picture of Christ and the church. Genesis 2-3 and Ephesians 5 are two of the most studied passages when it comes to marriage, but don't limit yourself to those popular texts. Look at the gospels, 1 Corinthians 7, the Song of Solomon, Ecclesiastes, 1 Peter, Proverbs, and a stack of other scripture passages that speak about what a Godly marriage between a man and a woman looks like. But don't go into it alone, like I said earlier, use other books, other pastors, and other married men to help you understand what these passages are talking about, and we'll get into a lot of those passages later in the book.

So when does this planning and preparation need to start? Hopefully, it already has, whether you know it or not. The first place we see a marriage is in our own parents, and that's true even if you've only known your parents to be unmarried, divorced, or widowed. The way a parent talks about their spouse, acts toward them, and serves them all shape the way that a child views relationships and marriage.

It's no wonder that people always expect to "turn into their parents." Our parents are our first, and most important, role model. So as we grow up, we are learning and preparing for marriage simply by what we experience. Conversely, men should be aware that they are teaching their children every second of every day. The thing you said to your wife was also said to your children. The way you acted toward your wife was also acted toward your children, good or bad. That is one reason that it is imperative to be in the Word on a regular basis. It can either encourage you to continue in the way of the Lord, as your parents taught you, and give fuller understanding to the lessons you have learned your whole life, or it can correct misconceptions, redirect your path, and teach you truth when nobody else has before. And don't just read it and then toss it aside. Really think about it and examine yourself in light of it so you can go into your marriage feeling good about your preparation.

When Lindsey and I were planning our wedding, we did some things to prepare, but I don't think I ever really examined myself or carefully thought about the things I was reading and hearing. We read and discussed *The Mystery of Marriage* by Mike Mason, and it was a great book, but I sort of read it just to read it, I didn't think all that much about it. And when we would discuss it together, I would give surface-level answers that probably didn't accomplish much as far as our preparation. We did pre-marital counseling with the pastor who married us, and again I'm afraid I didn't take it as seriously as I could have. Don't get me wrong, these things weren't worthless by any means, I did learn about marriage and how to be a husband and things like that, but I just filed them away in the back of my mind instead of actively trying to incorporate them into my life, which would soon become our life. And that became a problem for us. Like a lot of guys, I didn't know much about being a husband when I got married, so I had unmet expectations, difficulty communicating, confusion about my role in the marriage, and just a general sense that our marriage was not looking how it should. I had the books, I had done the counseling, so why wasn't this working out the way I thought it should? Granted, some of it was because of the fact that, like I said earlier, marriage is hard and you don't really know how to do it until you're in it. I get that, and it's true, but some of it was also because I had not truly decided to be prepared in my heart for our life together. I had gone through the motions doing what I was supposed to do without thinking about why I was supposed to do it.

Perhaps you are one of those men who find yourself in the position I was in then. Already married, but with no idea about what that should be like. Maybe you've even been married for a while and you're wondering if there's any way a chapter about preparation can apply to you. Well, it can. When a football coach gets a few games into his season and realizes that what he's doing isn't working, he goes back to the drawing board to develop a new plan. He looks at what has gone wrong, what has gone right, and how things are or are not working together. He changes direction so that his team, hopefully, can be successful from then on. If your marriage isn't working the way you think God wants it to, then get back to the drawing board and start planning. What is or isn't working? What are you going to do about it? What does the Bible say about it? Is counseling needed? Is confession and forgiveness needed? Or is it just a lot of little misunderstandings that need to be cleared up? There is absolutely no shame in admitting that things are not what they should be, because by turning to God and seeking His direction you can create a plan that will redirect your marriage onto a path that glorifies Christ. And the tools of planning are the same as they are for the unmarried man. Get into the Word, study what it says about your situation and your marriage, talk to your pastor, talk to other men, listen to sermons, and do all the things you can to change your mindset and create a plan that will restore your marriage to one that glorifies God and is a proper picture of Christ and his church. It probably won't happen overnight, but at least you'll have a plan that will get you there in the end.

There are also guys who are married and are doing really well. The marriage is going well, their relationship with their wife is strong, and Christ is guiding them. The planning and preparation then turn to this question: How are you going to keep it that way? Just letting it go is not going to be enough. How are you going to continue to grow? How are you going to keep things new and exciting? How can you continue to show your wife you love her? There are two main traps that guys fall into when things are going well. First, they don't recognize when things change and aren't going as well as they used to. It's common to hear a husband say, "I thought things were going well, I didn't know there was anything wrong!" You have to stay in tune with your wife and make sure, when things are going well, that they continue to go well. In fact, when things are going well may be the most important time to stay in tune with your wife and make sure you know what's working so you can keep doing that and make sure it stays that way. The second trap guys can fall into is that they stop doing the things that made them successful. With everything working, their Bible reading falls by the wayside, their prayer time diminishes, or they don't go to their pastor or other guys as much as they used to. With everything going well, why would they need to? But this is a common mistake among many people. We turn to God when we're crying, but forget about Him when we're smiling. But God is not there to pick you up when you're down only to have you run away and forget about him until you trip again. He needs to always be in the center of everything we do. Get in the Word, pray, be in community, and do it with the idea that you are never done learning and preparing to be a good husband.

And now the biggest question: Why should we do all of this planning and preparing? What are the benefits? Will it really make that much of a difference? Believe me, it will. There are a lot of benefits to preparing for marriage. The biggest one is that it will open your heart to follow God. By studying scripture, praying, and being in community with believers, you will not only learn about marriage but about your entire life, and you will want to honor God in everything. When our marriage and our home reflect Christ, the rest of our lives begin to reflect Christ as well. Another benefit is that it will show your wife that you are taking the marriage seriously and not just as something you'll try out to see if it fits. In a society where the majority of marriages end in divorce, you will be showing her that you want to learn and plan for a lifetime together, and that will make her feel more secure about the man she has decided to marry. Another benefit is that you will hopefully avoid some surprises. Not all of them, of course, because there are bound to be surprises anytime you start a new life with somebody, but expectations will be realistic and discussed together, future plans will have already been agreed on, and you'll start your marriage moving forward together with understanding, rather than feeling your way along a dark hallway.

Let me quickly give one last important idea about this whole topic. There is a fine line between planning and worrying, and the latter is something that we definitely should not burden ourselves with. In Matthew 6:25-34, Jesus tells us:

> Therefore I tell you, do not be anxious about your life,
> what you will eat or what you will drink, nor about your
> body, what you will put on. Is not life more than food,
> and the body more than clothing? Look at the birds

of the air: they neither sow nor reap nor gather into barns, and yet your heavenly Father feeds them. Are you not of more value than they? And which of you by being anxious can add a single hour to his span of life? And why are you anxious about clothing? Consider the lilies of the field, how they grow: they neither toil nor spin, yet I tell you, even Solomon in all his glory was not arrayed like one of these. But if God so clothes the grass of the field, which today is alive and tomorrow is thrown into the oven, will he not much more clothe you, O you of little faith? Therefore do not be anxious, saying, "What shall we eat?" or "What shall we drink?" or "What shall we wear?" For the Gentiles seek after all these things, and your heavenly Father knows that you need them all. But seek first the kingdom of God and his righteousness, and all these things will be added to you. Therefore do not be anxious about tomorrow, for tomorrow will be anxious for itself. Sufficient for the day is its own trouble.

Plan, prepare, learn, grow, and study, but do not worry. God has been gracious and faithful in giving us multiple ways to seek His path for our life, but sometimes His path is difficult to recognize. Or we think we see His path clearly, only to discover that He had something totally different in mind. So while it is important to have plans and prepare for the future, ultimately our life is in God's hands, and faithfulness to Him is what we should strive for above all else. That's not to say that planning is worthless, or that if we do plan that we are not trusting God. Indeed, the Bible tells us to plan, as noted earlier. It's simply a matter of being faithful to God and being a good steward of everything He gives us. The moment you start worrying about it is the moment that you have taken control for yourself instead of planning while knowing God is always in control.

So get that game plan ready. Plan and prepare to be close with God and to honor your wife. Show her that you love her enough to start being a good husband before you ever actually become one. And if things don't work out the way you thought? Don't worry, as long as you are faithful to God, they're working out the way that He thought.

As Your Wife's Quarterback...
You Need to be Her Leader.

It is without a doubt one of the most difficult positions in all of sports. Of course, there are the obvious reasons that being a quarterback is difficult, like the fact that he has to throw a ball at top speed or with perfect touch 30-50 times a game, or that at any moment before release he can get hit by a lineman moving like a pickup truck and weighing about the same. But beyond those physical things that we see so often, think about what a quarterback has to do. He has to inspire confidence in his teammates, more so than any other position. He has to believe that he can win the game at all times, effectively communicate with his teammates, make quick decisions, and forget failure easily, among many other things. But all of those attributes and characteristics fall under one simple umbrella: The quarterback needs to be the leader of the team. Almost every offensive play depends on him more than anyone else. He needs to be prepared more than anyone else. He needs to accept responsibility more than anyone else. Men, as your wife's quarterback, you need to be her leader.

Let's take a minute to recognize right away that this is a difficult, sensitive topic. Some women bristle at the idea of a man leading her, and some men cower at the responsibility of leading while other men try to be a leader but have no idea what a good leader looks like. But make no mistake, the husband as the head and leader of the family is exactly how God intended things to be, and I believe that if married couples live out these ideas in a Biblical, God-honoring way, they will discover true joy in each other and in Christ. Piles of books have been written on this topic and others like it, so if this is something you would like to study more in depth, I encourage you to read more and engage in conversation with other men and especially a pastor who can guide you through the scriptures so that you can continue to learn about how to be a proper, God-honoring leader in the home. For now, consider this chapter a taste of this subject.

When some members of the early church were having trouble figuring out the proper roles of men and women, Paul wrote in 1 Corinthians 11:3, "But I want you to understand that the head of every man is Christ, the head of a wife is her husband, and the head of Christ is God." That seems pretty straightforward. The wife is subject to the husband, who is subject to Christ, who is subject to God. But why is it that way? Where does that order come from? Paul answers that question as well just a few sentences later when he says, "For man was not made from woman, but woman from man. Neither was man created for woman, but woman for man" (1 Corinthians 11:8-9). Wives are not subject to husbands because the author of these verses is male, and it's not because men have an innate need for power. The reason that wives are subject to husbands is because that is how God created things to be.

Genesis 1 tells us that God said, "Let us make man in our image, after our likeness. And let them have dominion over the fish of the sea and over the birds of the heavens and over the livestock and over all the earth and over every creeping thing that creeps on the earth...Be fruitful and multiply and fill the earth and subdue it and have dominion over the fish of the sea and over the birds of the heavens and over every living thing that moves on the earth" (vs. 26,28). So God created people to *be in charge*. He wanted them to work the land, take care of the plants and animals, and just generally nurture the earth and everything in it, which he had given to them. Genesis 2 tells the more specific story of the creation of man after Genesis 1's overview, and in that chapter Adam is created first, and God puts him in Eden "to work it and keep it" (v. 15). Eve is not created until verse 22. So the ideas of dominion over the land and the responsibility to work the land and take care of it were given to Adam before Eve ever entered the picture. And why was Eve created in the first place? Because God had declared that "It is not good that the man should be alone; I will make him a helper fit for him" (v. 18). Eve was created to be Adam's helper, which implies that Adam was still the one who had the first responsibility given by God, and Eve was there to assist him and complement him as he carried out God's instructions. She was not there to be a simple laborer. She had a special job that only she could carry out, and Adam was to treat her as a special partner while still carrying out his responsibility to be the keeper of the earth.

So the leadership role has applied to the husband since the creation of man, and it has also applied to the quarterback since the creation of football. Both are very important and carry many of the same characteristics. I have identified eight of them to illustrate the connection.

1. A Good Quarterback Believes He Can Win and Inspires Confidence In His Team.

In one of the most famous upsets in NFL history, Super Bowl III ended with the New York Jets, as 18-point underdogs, defeating the Baltimore Colts 16-7. The story is known well to football fans as "The Guarantee." Three days before the game, Jets quarterback Joe Namath told the audience at the Miami Touchdown Club, "We're gonna win the game. I guarantee it." Most people felt this was ridiculous. The Jets were the clearly inferior team from the clearly inferior league. For Namath to guarantee victory over the superior Colts seemed to be wishful thinking that didn't have a chance of coming true. But the Jets beat the Colts because they believed they could. They prepared for the game like they could win instead of being resigned to the fact that everyone else thought they would lose. No doubt a large reason for that was because Namath, their quarterback and their leader, believed in them. He showed confidence in his whole team and believed that they could win, and he made them believe it too. One of the things a great quarterback does is inspire confidence in his team. If the quarterback seems resigned to losing, it trickles down to the rest of the team. If their leader doesn't believe they're good enough to win, why should they believe it? This is not to say that we should guarantee victory every time, but at least that we believe we can win every time. This shows the rest of the team that there is a goal worth working toward, and more importantly that the quarterback himself is going to work hard to reach that goal.

Another famous story occurs in 1 Samuel 17 when a young shepherd named David goes to battle with a mighty warrior named Goliath. It has become so popular that it is almost a pop culture cliché, but what a lot of people miss about that story is that not only did David defeat

Goliath, but he *knew he would*. When speaking to King Saul about the battle, David calmly tells him, "The LORD who delivered me from the paw of the lion and from the paw of the bear will deliver me from the hand of this Philistine" (v. 37) and when facing Goliath, David tells him, "You come to me with a sword and with a spear and with a javelin, but I come to you in the name of the LORD of hosts, the God of the armies of Israel, whom you have defied. This day the LORD will deliver you into my hand, and I will strike you down and cut off your head. And I will give the dead bodies of the host of the Philistines this day to the birds of the air and to the wild beasts of the earth, that all the earth may know that there is a God in Israel, and that all this assembly may know that the LORD saves not with sword and spear. For the battle is the LORD's, and he will give you into our hand" (vs. 45-47). David's confidence in his victory almost jumps off the page, and of course a few minutes later David was indeed holding Goliath's head after cutting it from his body. That kind of confidence inspired everyone in Israel to follow David's leadership.

One thing to remember is that we need to be confident we can win, not that we will win every time. In another famous Bible story in Daniel 3, Shadrach, Meshach, and Abednego refuse to bow to the king's golden idol and are threatened with being thrown into the fiery furnace. Facing this consequence, they tell the king, "If this be so, our God whom we serve is able to deliver us from the burning fiery furnace, and he will deliver us out of your hand, O king. But if not, be it known to you, O king, that we will not serve your gods or worship the golden image that you have set up" (vs. 17-18). Those three men were confident that God *could* give them the victory, not necessarily that he *would*. They knew that the victory would be the Lord's whether they died in the furnace or not, and the Lord saved them from the flames.

The same principle holds with our wives and families. We must inspire confidence in them so that they feel good about the person who is leading them. Again, we should not guarantee victory every time, nor should our wives expect it, but they should expect that we will work hard to reach the goal every time, whether it is fixing the broken washing machine, providing financial stability, or finding someone to watch the kids this weekend. No matter the situation, our wives should be confident that we will work hard to reach the goal, that they can count on us to do so, and that more often than not we will succeed in our goal. And even if we don't succeed that time, our wives will know that we tried our best and will continue to try our best the next time.

So how can we inspire such confidence? Simply by showing them that they can be confident in us. When a goal is set or a task needs to be performed, show your wife that you will work hard, and she will gain confidence as she sees you constantly trying to do the best you can. Joe Namath guaranteed that his team would win the game, but surely those words alone did not inspire his teammates. They had won eleven games that year and lost only three. Namath had been working hard all season long, and every week was prepared to lead his team to victory. They had seen it before, and no doubt they saw it again during preparations for the Super Bowl. Joe Namath didn't just tell his team that he believed they could win. He proved it. And that gave them confidence.

2. A Good Quarterback Gets His Team to Want to Follow Him.

A quarterback cannot force his team to believe in him, to have confidence in him, or to follow him as he leads. He cannot take his receivers, linemen, running backs, defense, and everyone else into a huddle and tell them, "I demand that you have the desire to follow me! You have to want to follow me or you're off the team!" It just doesn't work that way. You cannot force someone else to have a certain desire or emotion. But if a team does not want to follow its leader, the likelihood that the team will be successful is very slim. But, again, that desire to follow cannot be coerced or forced. So how does a quarterback get his team to want to follow him? The key comes in two parts: How he treats them and how he acts.

A quarterback who wants his team to follow him must treat his teammates respectfully. If he acts condescending toward them or tends to be aloof and ignore them, they will not respect him and will have no desire to follow him. He also must care about his teammates, which sometimes means to show compassion and offer help, and sometimes means to get in their face and challenge them to do better. Either way, the quarterback is showing that he cares about his teammates and what is going on in their games and in their lives. The team will see that and know that this is a man who is worth following because of how he treats them.

But direct contact is not the only time the team will observe what the quarterback is doing. This is why it is so important for the quarterback to be aware of how he is acting all the time. The best quarterbacks lead by example. Not only does the team see him acting respectfully and caring about his teammates, but they see him working in the weight room, studying his playbook, watching film, taking extra reps during practice, and not stopping until he knows he can do it right. The team sees this and knows that their leader is a hard worker who wants to succeed and that he will demand the same work ethic of himself that he demands of his teammates. It is when a quarterback questions his teammates' desire and then leaves practice early that respect is lost and the desire to follow dissolves.

The same principles apply to our relationship with our wives. Ephesians 5 tells us, "Husbands, love your wives, as Christ loved the church and gave himself up for her, that he might sanctify her, having cleansed her by the washing of water with the word, so that he might present the church to himself in splendor, without spot or wrinkle or any such thing, that she might be holy and without blemish" (vs. 25-27). The point in this passage is a kind of servant leadership where the husband sacrifices for his wife and considers her ahead of himself while still being the leader of the family. We need to care for our wives, not boss them around.

A few verses earlier, wives are told to submit to their husbands, but how can we desire that she follow us as her leader when we really do not give her a good reason to follow us at all? Does she feel respected and cared for or does she feel marginalized and shunned? If it is the latter, how can she be expected to want to follow a man who makes her feel that way? But knowing that her husband loves her, cares about her, and respects her will cause her to gladly follow him as the leader of the house because she knows that he will not act selfishly but with her and the family at the front of his mind. If this is a regular pattern of how her husband acts, she will feel safe expecting it.

How we act outside of direct contact with our wives has just as big of an impact on her desire to follow us as well. Just like the team sees the quarterback working hard physically and mentally, our wives must see us working hard in every aspect of our lives. Whether it be at our everyday jobs, fixing things around the house, trying to grow in knowledge and understanding, or continuing to challenge ourselves with new ideas, our wives will see us leading by example and will want to follow a husband who demands a lot of himself. Of course, one of the most important ways we need to lead by example is in our spiritual lives. This is the most common place that hypocrisy develops, and it is also most damaging. Do our wives and families see us taking our relationship with the Lord seriously, or is it an afterthought that only comes up on Sunday mornings? Do we strive to follow the Lord and obey Him in all we do, or is honoring God something that only comes up when the kids aren't doing what we want? Do we personally take time to memorize scripture, read the Bible, and pray, or are those things just done as a quick "thank you" before a meal or a bridge to bedtime? If following the Lord is not of importance in our life, make no mistake, our wives will see it, and it will not inspire them to follow us, or the Lord, themselves. Our example is paramount to our wives' spiritual lives. Remember that Ephesians 5 said that we are to present our wives without spot or wrinkle, but how can we do that if we do not encourage our wives to grow in their faith and give them an example of how to do so?

We may want our wives to follow us, but we have to show them why they should want to, instead of just expecting that they will.

3. A Good Quarterback Effectively Communicates With His Team.

On just about every single play of a football game, the quarterback is responsible for telling his team what play is going to be run at that moment. If he forgets, or tells them the wrong thing, or they misunderstand what he is saying, chances are that play is not going to be very successful. With some of the complicated offensive plays that are run in the NFL, including multiple options and variations, even the slightest miscommunication between the quarterback and his team can lead to failure on that play, from a simple no gain to a turnover returned for a touchdown. It is imperative that the quarterback communicate effectively with his team to increase the chances of success.

One year at the high school where I teach, the quarterback of our football team had been adopted from another country when he was young. Because of this, he had an accent that could make him difficult to understand, especially with the odd jargon of football plays. This could have led to a lot of confusion and broken plays, but every week before gameday his best friend on the team would go over to his house and listen to him call each play. If his friend couldn't understand it or heard the wrong thing, he would repeat it until he was able to say it clearly. They would even turn on loud music on the stereo to simulate outside noise so he would have to yell it and still make sure he could be understood.

It would have been easy for this young man (as it is for a lot of high school students, not to mention most men in our society) to eventually say, "Okay, that's fine. That's good enough." But he didn't say that. He worked and worked until he knew that there would be no question from his teammates about what play he was calling. He did not just get "close enough" with his communication skills, because "close enough" could be the difference between a win and a loss. No, he wanted to make sure that his team understood perfectly what he said and what play he was calling so that they could win the game.

For a Biblical example of this, go back to Adam and Eve. Genesis 3 gives us the account of the fall of man, and even further illuminates the point that Adam was to guide Eve and take responsibility for her. Notice first of all the command that God gave to Adam when He put Adam in Eden in chapter 2: "You may surely eat of every tree of the garden, but of the tree of the knowledge of good and evil you shall not eat, for in the day that you eat of it you shall surely die" (vs. 16-17). Now look at what Eve tells the serpent when explaining God's command in chapter 3: "You shall not eat of the fruit of the tree that is in the midst of the garden, neither shall you touch it, lest you die" (v. 3). Immediately, we can see the difference. Not only does Eve not mention the tree specifically by name (though we know, of course, that it turned out to be the same tree), but God did not say anything to Adam about touching the fruit. Clearly Eve knew of the command, so why the discrepancy? Did God tell Eve something different than He told Adam? That is doubtful. He would not have told Adam not to eat it and then a few days later decide, "Oh, you probably shouldn't touch it either, let's add that to the list." Did Eve simply misremember what God told her? Again, this is doubtful, since it was a pretty straightforward command in the first place. "Don't eat it or you'll die" seems easy to remember and hard to screw up. So what happened? Most likely, Adam was charged with leading Eve in the way of the Lord, and so he had to tell her about the command that God had given him when he was placed in the garden. I imagine a scenario in which Adam tells Eve not to eat the fruit of the tree, and then in a moment of embellishment tells her not even to touch it. It seems like the same way that someone would talk to a child, telling them to look both ways before they cross the street, and actually don't even step into the street to avoid the whole thing altogether. But the point for us here is not that Eve misquoted God, but rather that it was Adam's responsibility to communicate to her, and he did not do it correctly. He embellished and changed God's command, allowing the serpent an opening to tempt Eve. There's no way to know if the scene would have gone differently if Adam would have communicated correctly,

Communicating is unfortunately not seen in our culture as a characteristic of a man. Real men do not "talk," we are told. They do not share their feelings, discuss their emotions, or open up to anybody, because that would be seen as a sign of weakness. This is perhaps the greatest tragedy that we have cast onto relationships. How many marriages could have been saved if the people involved could have simply told the other what was wrong, why they were unhappy, or realized that by communicating with each other so many misunderstandings could be avoided? As husbands, we must be able to communicate with our wives on multiple levels to make sure that there is no confusion, no misunderstanding, and success can be achieved.

The first type of communication between spouses is what I call "Logistical Communication." This is one of the simplest forms of communication, but often the easiest to mess up. This includes daily activities and just making sure everyone is clear about how the practical events of life will unfold. Who will pick up the kids? Who will make dinner? When are we supposed to be at that party? What type of gift should we buy? Where does this item belong? These seem like such simple things, and they are, but often they are a cause of the most frustration in a relationship for two reasons: First, because of the simple nature of these things, we don't feel like there should ever be confusion or misunderstanding about them, so when there is we get angry. Second, since these things are such common, everyday questions, when they are not communicated effectively, it happens a lot, and it builds into a constant frustration. Then we start expecting the frustration, which is frustrating, and when it comes we add the new frustration to our existing frustration and get even more frustrated. It's not pretty.

Logistic communication also includes being clear about when you will carry out necessary tasks. Do not just tell your wife that you will fix the doorknob "sometime in the next few weeks." Not only does this increase her irritation with the doorknob with every day that goes by and it does not get fixed, but it does not give you any incentive to fix it. But if you tell her, "I may have time on Friday, but we also have something else going on that night, so if I don't have time to do it on Friday, I will definitely be able to do it the next Monday." That clear communication gives your wife confidence that it will be done when you say it will (if you are good at that in general), and as Tuesday,

Wednesday, and Thursday go by she will not get irritated with the doorknob because she knows that you are hoping to fix it on Friday, and even if it doesn't get done that day you are definitely going to do it the next Monday. That clear communication alleviates nagging and irritation for your wife and keeps you from being forgetful and lazy.

The second type of communication between spouses is "Emotional Communication." This is the one that makes most guys want to grab a drink and turn on a game of any kind. It is also the one that is the most important to a marriage. Forget what our culture tells you, forget what the guys at that bar say, forget what you see on TV and in movies. Real men are not the ones who put on a fake bravado and act like they have no emotions. Real men are the ones who can talk about their feelings with their wife and use that communication to build a stronger marriage. The men of the Bible were not afraid to show their emotions. The Psalms are full of examples of passionate emotions ranging from love to anger to wonder to helplessness. In the Song of Solomon the husband extols his wife's virtues and describes how much he loves her, and Jesus openly wept when his friend died. It is not unmanly to show our emotions, it is necessary to grow with and learn to love our wives.

Only by showing each other what is important to them, why it is important, and how they feel they can be cared for will a husband and wife learn how to truly love their spouse. Sure, you could get through your entire marriage by dodging questions, giving vague answers, and ignoring your emotions, but what kind of marriage is that? Does it abound in love? Does it make your wife feel special? Most importantly, does it honor God by being the kind of marriage He designed? No, it will be exactly the kind of marriage that too many people struggle with in our society. Cold, superficial, distant, and more a matter of convenience than of love.

Men, do not be a quarterback who expects his team to just know what the play is without telling them specifically. You must communicate with your wife and make sure that she understands you. It may take a lot of work and be difficult at first, but just as that high school quarterback called the plays over and over until he could be understood, you can work hard at communicating effectively and give your team the greatest chance for success.

4. A Good Quarterback Changes the Plan If Necessary.

There is a moment as the quarterback steps to the line of scrimmage that he surveys the defense and in one, quick look gets a pretty good idea of whether the play that has been called should succeed or will likely fail. Of course, he is not always right, there are a lot of factors that determine if a play gains 12 yards or -3, but the quarterback can usually recognize if the play that has been called will work against the defense he is now looking at. If he thinks not, he gets the attention of his teammates and calls an audible, changing the play to something else that he thinks will work better. Maybe he changes from a run play to a pass play, or maybe he changes from going left to going right. Whatever the case, he is trying to put his team in the best position to gain yards and be successful. When most people think of quarterbacks who call a lot of audibles, they think of Peyton Manning of the Denver Broncos. Manning is well known to change the play after the huddle, and it's hard to argue with the results. So far, he has won the NFL MVP award four times (the most of any player in league history), was Super Bowl MVP when the Colts won the title in 2007, and holds 45 NFL regular season individual records along with 12 NFL postseason individual records and 7 NFL rookie records. He is without a doubt one of the most successful quarterbacks of all time, and part of that success is due to the fact that he is one of the best ever at being able to change his plan to something that will be more successful. In a matter of seconds, Manning (and all quarterbacks, of course, but he is one of the best at it) comes out of the huddle, reads the defense, and decides if the play that has been called will work or if there is a better option. If he wants to change it, he immediately decides on a new play and communicates it to his teammates quickly so everyone knows the new plan. That ability has made him one of the best quarterbacks in NFL history.

In the chapter about being your wife's head coach, we talked about planning. Planning is definitely an important aspect of our lives and our relationships, but inevitably there will be changes that need to be made. As we plan for and with our wives, we need to be constantly reading the situation and ready to change the plan if we have to. A quarterback does not come out of the huddle and run the play that was called without looking at what the defense is doing. He immediately starts looking for possible roadblocks, and if he sees any he starts thinking about how to avoid them. The same is true for us as husbands. As we make our plans and try to carry them out, roadblocks will present themselves. Some will be products of our own poor planning or lack of good decision making, and some will be unavoidable circumstances of life. Either way, those roadblocks need to be avoided or at least dealt with. That is why we need to be constantly ready to evaluate our plans and our progress, and accept the fact that we may need to change the plan to be more successful in the long run.

There is one other option that a quarterback has if he doesn't think the current plan will succeed: He can call a timeout. Sometimes this is our best option. Instead of trying to force a plan that is unfamiliar or just hope that whatever happens ends up being positive, the quarterback can stop everything and regroup with his team on the sideline to take some time and come up with a new plan. Sometimes our plan in life gets so off track or the roadblocks look so daunting that we just need to stop everything, step back for a bit, and regroup to figure out a new plan. But just like in a football game, our timeouts cannot last forever. Eventually we need to get back into the game and keep moving forward.

Finally, think about who on the field changes the play or calls timeout. It is the quarterback, every time. Other players do not decide to call timeout or yell out a new play to the rest of the offense. It is the quarterback's responsibility alone, and as the leaders of our families, it is our responsibility to recognize obstacles to our plan and make the appropriate changes. Every player on the offense looks to the quarterback to lead them, and our families should look to us to do the same.

5. A Good Quarterback Makes Quick Decisions During the Play.

A quarterback may have a few quick seconds to read a defense and change the play after coming out of the huddle, but he has even less time than that to make decisions after the play starts. When the ball is snapped, 21 other large and fast men start running around and banging into each other, and in the midst of all that the quarterback must see everything that is going on and make a decision based on all of it. Should he hand off the ball or keep it himself? Which receiver should he throw to? How long should he wait to throw or hand off? How quickly should he throw it? All of these and so much more are decided in the quarterback's head in a split second. Any wrong decision could lead to failure, and he cannot avoid it. A decision must be made.

The same idea applies to husbands as we lead our wives. Sometimes we are going to need to make quick decisions as the "play" is happening, and we cannot avoid it. We cannot run or hide from these decisions, we must face them and do something about it. Understandably, these are the hardest decisions to make, and will probably result in failure some of the time, but often the failures of these quick decisions are not crippling. If a quarterback makes a bad decision, the ball may drop incomplete, or the ball carrier may be tackled for a loss. In those cases the offense immediately gets to try again with a new play. You may experience some of those small failures, but rest assured that you will get another chance. One hard decision in the heat of the moment should not prevent you from regrouping and trying again. In a relatively rare instance, the defense may take the ball away or even score, but unless it is the last possession of the game, the offense will always get another chance. Those are the times in your life when timeouts can be helpful so you can reassess the situation and decide the best way to move forward from where you now find yourself.

Of course, the Bible speaks a lot about being discerning and not making hasty decisions, but what we're talking about here is not being hasty, it's making a quick decision when necessary. It is always better to be thoughtful and seek the Lord's will, but sometimes that's just not possible and a quick decision needs to be made. The key is that we are following the Lord consistently throughout our daily lives, so that when the decision needs to be made quickly, we can do it with a focus on the Lord because that's where our focus always is.

6. A Good Quarterback is Willing to Hand Off the Ball.

As we have established, the quarterback is probably the most important offensive player on the field and has the most influence on almost every play his team runs. It is very rare for an offense to run a play that does not involve the quarterback touching the ball. But how many plays *end* with the quarterback holding the ball as well? Very few. An average

NFL team runs over 1,000 plays over the course of the regular season, but the vast majority of them consist of the quarterback giving the ball to somebody else. In 2010, Peyton Manning, described earlier as one of the most successful quarterbacks in the history of the league, kept the ball only 18 times. In fact, Michael Vick of the New York Jets, considered one of the best running quarterbacks in league history, kept the ball 100 times during the 2010 regular season. The next highest number was only 68 by Josh Freeman, at the time with the Tampa Bay Buccaneers. So the quarterback who kept the ball the most in the league (and almost twice as often as the next closest) still gave it to one of his teammates about 90% of the time. He is still leading the team and is most responsible for the team's success, but very rarely is he the guy advancing the ball.

This is a hard thing for people in our culture to learn. Success is not reliant only on ourselves and what we do, there are many other people who want to help us and work with us to help us succeed. As leaders, we need to be willing to hand off the ball. We don't have to do everything ourselves, and we certainly don't need to stop people from helping us. We often need to let go, let someone else run with it, and succeed as a team.

This lesson even came up for the early church soon after Jesus ascended to Heaven. Acts 6 tells the story of how the church was growing very quickly, and became so large that it was difficult to take care of every detail. The twelve apostles were in charge for obvious reasons, but a problem came up because not everyone in the church was being taken care of like they should have. Certain poor widows were not getting what they needed for various reasons, but one reason is that the apostles simply could not handle the responsibility of preaching the word and spreading the new gospel while at the same time overseeing the distribution to the members of the church. Instead of trying to do everything themselves and making it even worse, they told the whole church, "Therefore, brothers, pick out from among you seven men of good repute, full of the Spirit and of wisdom, whom we will appoint to this duty. But we will devote ourselves to prayer and to the ministry of the word" (vs. 3-4). The twelve apostles knew that they couldn't handle everything on their own, so they turned it over to other people that they trusted and who loved the Lord. That way, both the physical needs and the spiritual needs of the church could be handled to the glory of God.

Handing off the ball looks different depending on the circumstances. Maybe you take up someone at work on their offer to finish the project on their own so you can go home and spend time with your family. Maybe you ask someone to take your spot volunteering because you know you're spreading yourself thin and not getting enough sleep. Maybe you allow your wife to design the kitchen remodel because you just don't know much about that. Regardless of circumstances, nobody can do 100% of the work by themselves and we have to ask for help sometimes. For me, it's a matter of money management. I'm really good at budgeting and keeping track of our spending, but for some reason I'm really bad at remembering to pay bills. I tend to get them in the mail or electronically, and then forget about them. I don't know where that disconnect comes from, but I know it's there, and so I asked my wife to take care of paying the monthly bills. She takes care of sending in the check for our mortgage and trash service, as well as going online to pay for our cell phones, electricity, student loans, and heat. She takes care of those things without fail every month, and I don't have to worry about them. I handed that off to her soon after we got married because I knew she was better at it than I was, and we have avoided late payments ever since, not to mention the marital tension that comes with spending money on late fees and interest.

Men, be the leader of your family and guide them toward success, but do not force yourself to do everything. Get help when you need it, defer to others who may be better suited for certain tasks, and trust your wife to take care of things that you don't want to worry about. It will keep you from wearing yourself out and allow you to have the energy and attitude you need to be a leader that your family wants to follow.

7. A Good Quarterback Learns From Failure and Moves On to the Next Game.

It's a well-known cliché in the sports world, one that we've heard time and time again as things don't go our team's way: "You can't win 'em all." It seems obvious enough. You try as hard as you can to win, but you're not going to win every time. Sometimes, you're going to lose. Everyone knows that. So why do we dwell on it? Why do we allow our losses to stay in our memory and eat at us? For some reason, we have a hard time forgetting about our losses and moving on. But, perhaps ironically, the people who find the most success are the ones who have best learned to deal with failure. Quarterbacks are no different. Every single time a game is played, a quarterback loses. But the real gauge of a quarterback is not only if he wins or loses, but how he responds to the losses.

If a quarterback, or anyone, allows himself to focus on his failure, either big or small, and cannot let go of it, he will never be able to completely focus on his next challenge. It is only when he can forget his failures of the past that he can move on and work hard to win the next time. Brett Favre is the winningest quarterback in NFL history with 186 victories and also holds numerous NFL records, including most career pass completions (6,300), most career passing yards (71,838), and most career passing touchdowns (508). Does that mean that Favre never experienced failure? Of course not. Favre also holds the record for most career interceptions (336), most career times being sacked (525), and has the second-most career losses (112). Also, Favre only won the Super Bowl one time, meaning that 19 of his 20 seasons either ended with a loss or not making the playoffs at all. And yet, Favre is considered one of the most successful quarterbacks in NFL history, and why? Because every time he lost a game, every time he threw an interception, and every time he got sacked, he could forget about it and focus on the next game, the next play, or the next season. He couldn't let it eat away at him, or he would not be able to focus on whatever came next.

It is inevitable. Sometimes, we will fail. They may be big failures or relatively small failures, but they will come. And just like the quarterback, the key is not how we fail or how often it happens, but how we respond to it. If we focus on our losses and see ourselves as someone who just fails a lot, then we are not learning and we are not allowing ourselves to move on and succeed the next time. But if we can learn from our failures, refocus on whatever comes next, and start working hard to succeed the next time, we allow ourselves to have a positive attitude and not dwell on the past.

Some of our failures are because of circumstances we can't control. Maybe you took a risk by lending money to somebody and they never paid you back, or maybe you weren't ready for a presentation because of computer problems, or maybe you had a financial plan for your family and then lost your job. Those things happen, and they are not your fault, so these types of failures can be easier to recover from emotionally. You will simply try something else, come up with a new plan, and move on with more knowledge than you had before.

It is much harder to recover emotionally from failures that occur because of our own sin. Maybe your marriage fell apart because you committed adultery, or maybe your family is in financial ruin because of your gambling problem, or maybe your uncontrolled anger led you to attack someone. It is so difficult to learn from these mistakes and move on because we know we are at fault, and the shame, depression, and anxiety they create do not allow us to move on and do better the next time. Jesus teaches about this in the familiar story from John 8:3-11:

> The scribes and the Pharisees brought a woman who had been caught in adultery, and placing her in the midst they said to him, "Teacher, this woman has been caught in the act of adultery. Now in the Law Moses commanded us to stone such women. So what do you say?" This they said to test him, that they might have some charge to bring against him. Jesus bent down and wrote with his finger on the ground. And as they continued to ask him, he stood up and said to them, "Let him who is without sin among you be the first to throw a stone at her." And once more he bent down and wrote on the ground. But when they heard it, they went away one by one, beginning with the older ones, and Jesus was left alone with the woman standing before him. Jesus stood up and said to her, "Woman, where are they? Has no one condemned you?" She said, "No one, Lord." And Jesus said, "Neither do I condemn you; go, and from now on sin no more."

The woman in this story has failed because of her sin. She has committed adultery. But Jesus does not cast her into Hell immediately, he forgives her of her sin and tells her to continue on, but with an important instruction: from now on, sin no more. Here is Jesus telling us that we do not need to dwell on the sins of our past, but with a renewed heart that wants to do what is right and succeed the next time. Perhaps you have committed a sin in your past that you are unable to let go of and you are still burdened by the sorrow it causes you. Know that in Jesus we are forgiven of our sins and we can take the lessons we have learned and move forward, working hard to find success in our next challenge.

Just as the quarterback does not dwell on his failures, but learns from them and moves forward, we can also learn from our failures and go on with a new sense of purpose, to succeed the next time.

8. A Good Quarterback Accepts Responsibility

There is another aspect to dealing with failure beyond just learning from it and moving on. If he throws an interception, fumbles the ball, or doesn't play well enough for his team to win the game, what does the good quarterback do? He takes responsibility for himself. He does not point fingers or cast blame on anyone else, and he does not run away and hide. He stands up and accepts responsibility for his decisions. This shows his teammates that he is a man of character, not trying to throw anyone else under the bus, but living out his role as the leader of the team and example for his teammates.

After a tough loss to the University of California, Stanford quarterback Andrew Luck sat in front of the media after the game and said, "I didn't make the plays when it counted...The blame falls on me" (San Francisco Chronicle, 11/22/09). Two years later, Luck was considered one of the best college quarterbacks in the country and a front-runner for the Heisman Award. In an interview with WEEI radio, Tom Brady of the New England Patriots, after a playoff loss to the New York Jets, admitted, "I really let the team down and didn't play the way I was capable." At the time, Brady had already won three Super Bowls, two Super Bowl MVP Awards, two NFL MVP Awards, and holds the record for most touchdown passes in a single season. With all of that on his resume', it would have been easy for Brady to say after that loss, "I'm Tom Brady. I'm one of the best quarterbacks in history. Get off my back." But he didn't say that. He accepted responsibility for what he knew was a sub-par performance, and he admitted it to his teammates and his fans.

But the ability to take responsibility is not something that comes easy. In fact, it seems like our first response is to point fingers and blame others, and it has been that way since the beginning. Think back to the story of Adam and Eve that we talked about earlier. When God finds them in the garden and asks what has happened, what does Adam do? He points the finger at Eve and blames her for his own sin against God. Adam did not take responsibility as the leader, and they suffered because of it. So being able to accept responsibility is something that we need to work on; don't expect it to come easily.

Of course, it's one thing to take responsibility for losing a game. It's quite another to take responsibility for personal failures, and especially our sin. It is not easy to admit that we have failed and sinned, but it is something we must do. In order to fully give our lives to God, we must admit to Him that we are sinners and that we cannot get away from our sin without Him. And when we fail, we must always confess our sins to God and ask his forgiveness. The problem is that, even though we know we must confess our sins to God, we often stop there. But most of the time our sin was not just against God, but against somebody else as well, and Jesus tells us that we must confess our sins to others and ask their forgiveness as well. In Matthew 5:23-24, he says, "So if you are offering your gift at the altar and there remember that your brother has something against you, leave your gift there before the altar and go. First be reconciled to your brother, and then come and offer your gift." Later, James 5:16 says, "Therefore, confess your sins to one another and pray for one another, that you may be healed." In both of these instances, confessing sins and asking for forgiveness is very important. So important, in fact, that we struggle in our relationship with God if we refuse to confess our sins and ask forgiveness of other people because God wants His followers to be in unity and to love each other as He loves us. When we don't do that, we are accepting the love of God without extending that love to anyone else.

Because of the large percentage of time you spend with her and sheer number of interactions you have with her, the person you will probably need to confess to the most is your wife. Whether for small sins, large sins, and everything in between, confessing your sin and asking your wife's forgiveness is absolutely essential to a healthy marriage. When we fall into blaming others, getting defensive, or running from our mistakes, there can be no growth and it destroys any trust that has been built. But telling our wives when we have failed and asking them to forgive us shows them that we are willing to take responsibility for ourselves and that we want to change, get better, and not sin any more. That will build trust and your wife will see you as a man who wants to improve himself and do whatever he can to love his wife completely.

Another benefit of confessing to your wife is that she will then be aware of the sins you struggle with, and will be able to help you. If you struggle with sexual sin, she will be able to help you stay away from temptation. If you struggle with money, she can be aware of that and help you set the budget and pay the bills. If you struggle with anger, she can help you recognize when you need to calm down. Whatever the problem is, making your wife aware of it will allow her to help you get whatever help you need and support you in your effort to become a better person.

Pointing fingers and blame shifting is a temporary solution to a much larger problem. By confessing your sins and asking forgiveness, you take responsibility for yourself and will allow yourself to become a leader that improves himself and shows his wife that he wants to be a better man.

* * *

It is one of the most difficult positions in sports, and also one of the most important. The quarterback is the leader of his team and is the person most responsible for their success. Men, get onto the field and be your family's quarterback. Be the leader that they want and need.

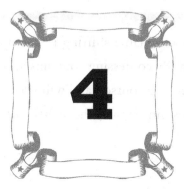

As Your Wife's Running Back...
You Need to be Her Worker.

During the 2012 NFL season, yardage totals for the top running backs and wide receivers were remarkably similar. The top ten running backs gained an average of 1,465 yards, with Adrian Peterson of the Minnesota Vikings leading everyone with 2,097 yards. The top ten wide receivers gained an average of 1,468 yards, with the Detroit Lions' Calvin Johnson leading the way at 1,964 yards. (It should be noted that Peterson and Johnson were both something of an anomaly that year as Johnson broke the single-season record and Peterson came nine yards away. Both also were about 400 yards ahead of their nearest competitor). So the total yardage for each position tends to be similar, but where the real difference lies is in how many times the players in those positions touch the ball, and of course along with that, their average yardage per play. Looking at it one way, the running back with the highest average yards per rush in 2012 was Peterson and Buffalo's

C.J. Spiller with 6.0 yards per carry, but 137 different qualified players averaged more than 6.0 yards per catch. Looking at it from the other direction, Johnson led the league with 122 catches, but 32 different players had at least 122 rushes during the season. The running back is the one who is asked to shoulder a difficult workload every game. The end results are about the same, but the running backs have to get the ball about three times as often for those same results. Sometimes they break off a big run, but most of their carries result in gains of 0-5 yards, and sometimes even negative yards. But still they take the ball and keep working. Men, as your wife's running back, you need to be her worker.

As established in the chapter on being your wife's Quarterback, you are in a position of authority in your marriage and family. You, as the husband, have been designed to sacrificially lead your family. That position certainly holds many responsibilities, including making hard decisions, planning the future, teaching and correcting, and many others, but one of the main responsibilities that God gives any person in a position of authority is to take care of those who are under them. As the authority, we are not simply to dictate what happens or demand that our needs are met. Instead, we are to lovingly care for the people under our authority as the Lord has called us to do. This includes both money and house care. And understand that this is not just a suggestion, this is something that God has commanded us to do as men. The most serious exhortation of this idea in the Bible is in 1 Timothy 5:8 when Paul writes, "But if anyone does not provide for his relatives, and especially for members of his household, he has denied the faith and is worse than an unbeliever." Clearly, this is not something that God takes lightly. He does not just say it is a matter of taking care of people and providing for them, but a matter of our faith itself. How can we claim to love the Lord and love our family as we ought to if we don't make any effort to take care of them? If we don't, we aren't just letting our family down, but we're actually denying the responsibility that God has given us, and therefore denying Him, which obviously is not a small matter. And notice in the verse that there is a small hierarchy being drawn about whom you should care for. First, the members of your own household, your wife and children. It makes very little sense to support and provide for someone outside of your immediate family if you are not caring for them first. Then comes other family members and, I believe, other brothers and sisters in Christ. We are to take care of each other as believers, like the early church did in Acts 2, or as it says in Galatians 6:10, "So then, as we have opportunity, let us do good to everyone, but especially to those who are of the household of faith."

One of the main reasons that we should take our job as worker seriously is because it allows us to be a representation of what God does for us. God takes care of us as His children, so we should take care of our family as well. Now this gets hard for some people, because not everyone feels like or believes that God has taken care of them. To that, we can say that God has taken care of all people by sending Jesus to die for our sins and thus open the way of salvation, so to say that God has not taken care of you is not true. With all of the problems in this world, the poor decisions we make, and how often we turn away, believe me, we are here because of God, not in spite of him. Perhaps you just need to recognize how God is taking care of you, instead of demanding that He do a better job. But the fact remains that He is taking care of you, and that means you also have a responsibility to take care of those under you. By providing for our wives and children, we are living out the reality that God takes care of us, and we are able to give Him the glory for everything. We can honestly say that it is God who gives us the opportunities to provide for our families, and even that it is still God doing the providing, just working through us in the way he has called us. By being that example, our wives and children will not only feel loved and cared for, but they will see an Earthly picture of their Heavenly Father who loves them and takes care of them, and that will help guide them into their own relationship with God.

Feeling loved and cared for is one of our basic human needs, and working for your family is one way to make them feel that way. When the rest of a football team sees the running back working hard and playing his hardest, even when he's only getting small gains, they know that he cares about the team and cares about winning. In the same way, when our wives see us working hard to provide for them as best we can, they know that we care about them and the whole family, and that it is important to us to provide for them. Obviously this doesn't mean that "more work=more love," there has to be a balance of various aspects of your life, and you can't show love in other ways if you're gone working all the time. Be aware of working a proper amount to provide for your family and spending time with them as well.

Another benefit to being an example of a Godly man to your family is that they will want to study and follow the role that God has for them as well. When we are serious about taking on the roles and responsibilities that God has given us, our wives will become serious about taking on the roles and responsibilities that God has given them. Not only will this produce a mutual love and respect in the relationship, but I believe it will also help families to understand, organize, and structure their lives. For as the husband is working to provide for his family, the wife is called to serve the family in a unique way by taking care of the house and staying with the kids if possible. How can she do that if her husband is not working and providing for his family? But remember that working a job to provide financially for the family does not absolve the husband of all responsibilities in the house. While it is true that the wife is generally responsible for the household, there are times when that job becomes very large. If there are children, the father is the primary teacher and leader for them, and so while it is the mother who is with them most of the day, the father must assume his role as teacher when he is home. Especially if the kids are having a particularly hard day, the mother may be at the end of her rope emotionally, and dad needs to step in to help out and give her a break. Or there may be times, for a variety of reasons, that things in the house back up a bit. The laundry is piled up, the sink is full of dishes, stuff is cluttered everywhere, the furniture is dusty, the floor needs vacuuming, and the list goes on. It's times like those when your wife needs some help, and serving her should come into play. Yes, you work hard all day to provide, but one of your other responsibilities is to love and serve your wife. We don't just grab a beverage, sit down in front of the TV, and say, "Wow, you have a lot of work to do. Good luck with that." We help how we can so that everything in the house can get back to a manageable state and our wives can continue doing their job joyfully instead of begrudgingly.

There are also a lot of tasks around the home that should fall into the husband's realm, and taking care of those things is something we should be watching for and doing in a timely manner. What those tasks are will differ with various situations and abilities, but there are always things that need to be done. In our house, I take on the outside jobs like mowing the lawn, raking the leaves, and shoveling snow. I also try to take care of anything that involves machines or any kind of "dirty" job like fixing the faucet or hooking up a water line in the basement (most anything in the basement is my job because my wife doesn't like to venture down there if she doesn't have to). So when the belt broke on our dryer, I replaced it. When the bathroom door swelled in the summer, I sanded it down. When the toilet wouldn't flush, I got it cleared up. These don't sound like big things, but to my wife, who spends most of her time at the house, they are a huge help, and it helps alleviate her frustration. Plus, I am not exactly the handiest man in the world, but that doesn't stop me from trying to take care of things around the house. Thank goodness for the internet and friends and family who know things, or I would be totally lost. Learning how to do something you didn't know and then coming through for your wife gives her another layer of respect for you, since she sees that you are not only a worker, but a problem solver, and that you care enough to actually go through the steps of learning something new. And then the next time it happens, or if someone you know needs help, you'll already know what you're doing. When the turn signal burned out on our minivan, I watched a few videos online and read a couple articles, then went out and changed that bulb myself. It took about fifteen minutes because it took me a bit to figure out how to get pieces out and then back in and how they fit together, but eventually I got it. Six months later, the turn signal on the other side burned out, so I grabbed the extra bulb and finished the job in about two minutes. Every time you learn something new, you're saving yourself time in the future.

Of course, you have to know the limits of your abilities. When our furnace stopped working (not a good problem to have when winter is approaching in Minnesota), I went downstairs, stared at it for a few seconds, then came back upstairs and e-mailed a friend who works on furnaces. He got it fixed the next day. When the engine burned out on our washing machine, I looked at it, then had my brother-in-law look at it, then had my mom's husband look at it, then I went out and bought a new washing machine. I'm sure that I could have learned how to fix the motor on a washing machine eventually, but probably not before I ran out of clothes.

Another thing to remember is that there may be times when the husband is unable to get work so his wife works to bridge the gap until he can find a job. Or maybe he is going through a training program to eventually get a job and his wife works in the meantime. When we first got married, I had one year left of graduate school to finish my teaching license. My wife had received a degree in meteorology with a minor in math, so she found a job that she did well and supported us financially for a year until I started teaching. Shortly after that, our first child was born, and she was able to quit her job and stay home as I was now working full-time. So, while the most ideal way to set up a family is for the husband to work and provide financial support while the wife takes on the responsibility of the household, there are certain reasons that it may not work for a while, or because there is an end goal in sight, or whatever the case may be. But there is no Biblical support for a husband just deciding not to have a job or provide for his family. If you are an able-bodied man, you should be working for your family.

There is one more reason I'd like to mention as to why a man should be working consistently. It is not because of his responsibility to his wife, but because of his responsibility to God. Over and over, the Bible tells us to avoid idleness and laziness because it can result in falling into temptation and not tending to the things that we should be taking care of. Laziness can even lead directly to sin. In verses like 2 Thessalonians 3:11 and 1 Timothy 5:13, Paul encourages his readers to not become idle because it can result in gossiping and meddling in other people's lives instead of taking care of our own business. Just before that, in 2 Thessalonians 3:6, Paul even says, "Now we command you, brothers, in the name of our Lord Jesus Christ, that you keep away from any brother who is walking in idleness..." Not only did Paul want them to stay away from idleness themselves, but he even warned them not to hang around people who are idle because it is easy to get sucked into that mindset.

Think about what happens when you're not making a point of working and using your time. Maybe you watch hours disappear on the TV or computer doing nothing of value. Or maybe you find yourself eating as the time goes by, and not vegetables either. Or maybe you just fall asleep on the couch and wake up hours later only to realize all the things you could have accomplished but didn't. Whatever the case, none of these things are inherently bad, and there need to be breaks taken from work, but they are bad when they consistently take the place of things that should be a higher priority, whether it's getting things done around the house, reading your Bible, job hunting, memorizing verses, studying, helping your wife, or spending time with your kids. And when we always turn to habits of idleness instead of habits of work, it becomes more difficult to do the work when we need to. If a running back shows up for practice every day but decides to watch TV instead of studying his playbook, or eat a little extra at mealtime instead of hitting the weight room, he certainly won't be ready to play when it's game time. And if we're lounging on the couch every day instead of being active and getting things done, we won't be ready to work when we really need to.

So get working, men. Grab the ball and continue to run, no matter how many times you're stopped for a short gain, because those short gains can add up to big numbers.

As Your Wife's Fullback...
You Need to be Her Servant.

Total yards. Touchdowns. Carrying the ball. Being in the spotlight. Racking up the stats. All of these things are what we are taught create the best players on the best teams. They are the things that are celebrated, and why shouldn't they be? Those things win games. They are exciting. And they make fans want to watch the game. It is not a surprise, then, when looking at decorated athletes, to find that (through 2013) the Heisman Trophy has been awarded to a quarterback, running back, or wide receiver 75 of 78 times (including earlier players listed as halfbacks or an earlier version of fullback). The Super Bowl MVP Award has been given to one of those three positions 39 of 49 times. The NFL season MVP Award has gone to one of those three positions 55 of 58 times (And, actually, those 55 winners have all been quarterbacks or running backs). In our culture, gaudy stats and huge wins equal awards and accolades. But ask most of those award-winners why they were so successful, and many, if not all, of them will say that their teammates had much to do with their success. This is especially true of running backs, who are very much reliant on others to succeed. If tacklers are not blocked, that running back isn't going anywhere, no matter how fast he is. It is common to hear about running backs buying gifts for teammates or taking them out to a fancy dinner because they had a successful season. And there is one position that serves the running back more than perhaps any other: the fullback. The fullback drives ahead of the running back, ready to block anyone and everyone out of the way so that the running back can get into the open field and do what he does best. His primary responsibility is to play for somebody else's success. He serves the running back without worrying about his own stats, his own accolades, or his own trophies.

One of the best fullbacks of all time was Lorenzo Neal. He played for seven different teams during his 16-year NFL career, but no matter where he played, behind his blocking, his team's running back broke 1,000 yards in eleven straight seasons. During the sixteen seasons in which he played, he gained only 807 yards and scored only six touchdowns. Not exactly awe-inspiring. But perhaps most telling about Neal were his two years with the Tennessee Titans. During the 1999 season, Neal carried the ball two times for one total yard. The following season, he carried the ball only one time for -2 total yards. But what did the Titans' running back, Eddie George, do? In those two seasons combined, he rushed for 2,813 yards and 23 touchdowns, and was named 1st Team All-Pro in both seasons. And it was not a coincidence that Lorenzo Neal was helping him. Neal took the field every week ready to do his job and serve however he could so that someone else could find success and be put in the spotlight. Men, as your wife's fullback, you need to be her servant.

Servanthood is not something that our culture admires or encourages. Putting someone else ahead of yourself is almost a foreign concept to many in our society. "Look out for yourself!" we're told, and "How can you love others without loving yourself first?" Actually, though, the only way you can truly learn to love yourself is by loving others first. Serving others is one of the greatest things we can do in this life, which is why it is a common theme throughout the Bible. It begins in the Garden of Eden, when Adam and Eve look first to their own interests and what they want, rather than serving God as he instructed them. Their impulse was to serve themselves, instead of serve God. After the people of Israel are led out of Egypt, God gives Moses the Ten Commandments (Exodus 20), which first tell us how to love and serve God, and then tell us how to serve each other. Jesus himself explains the whole law as being dependent on these two ideas. ""You shall love the Lord your God with all your heart and with all your soul and with all your mind. This is the great and first commandment. And a second is like it: You shall love your neighbor as yourself" (Matthew 22:37-39).

In fact, many of Jesus' teachings include the idea of servanthood. One of the most famous stories in the Bible is found in Luke 10, the Parable of the Good Samaritan. The Samaritan stops to help a man who has been robbed and beaten, and not only tends to his wounds and helps him to an inn where they can help him, but even pays for the man's care out of his own pocket. The story takes on even greater weight when Jesus implies that the two men who previously passed by the hurt man and did nothing will not inherit eternal life. Elsewhere in the gospels, Jesus tells the disciples in Mark 9:35, "And he sat down and called the twelve. And he said to them, 'If anyone would be first, he must be last of all and servant of all'" and similarly in Matthew 23:11-12,

"The greatest among you shall be your servant. Whoever exalts himself will be humbled, and whoever humbles himself will be exalted."

Not only did Jesus teach about servanthood, but set the example Himself. He tells His disciples explicitly in Mark 10:45, "For even the Son of Man came not to be served but to serve, and to give His life as a ransom for many." Jesus did not come to Earth to be placed on a throne or to have others attend His every need (And He certainly could have, since He is God, after all), but rather to take care of us, teach us, and ultimately die for us. One of the final lessons that Jesus taught His disciples was the night before He died. According to John 13, during supper, Jesus stood up, took off his outer garments, wrapped a towel around his waist, and proceeded to wash the disciples' feet. This was a job that was always done by the servants of the house. It was not a job that anyone would actually want to do. But there was Jesus doing it, and not to a King or a High Priest or anyone else of high social standing, but to His disciples, His friends, who called Him Lord. Peter recognized this and, when Jesus came to Him, refused to be washed. Jesus responded to Peter in verse 10, "If I do not wash you, you have no share with me" and then when He was finished told them all in verses 13-15, "You call me Teacher and Lord, and you are right, for so I am. If I then, your Lord and Teacher, have washed your feet, you also ought to wash one another's feet. For I have given you an example, that you also should do just as I have done to you." In His final full day before being crucified, one of Jesus' final lessons to us was to serve one another and take care of each other.

That story of Jesus washing the disciples' feet also foreshadows His ultimate act of servanthood the next day, His death on the cross. That night of the Last Supper, Jesus quite literally washed the dirt from His followers. The next day, His blood washed the dirt of sin from His followers. Remember that marriage is a picture of Christ and the church, where the church is the bride of Christ. Jesus, as the groom, does the "dirty work" and cleanses His bride with the washing of water with the word so that His bride can be presented spotless and blameless, without blemish, like Ephesians 5 says.

But the lesson of servanthood did not stop when Jesus ascended to Heaven. Paul wrote on the idea multiple times to different churches. He was very clear that we should look to serve others when he wrote in Galatians, "For you were called to freedom, brothers. Only do not use your freedom as an opportunity for the flesh, but through love serve one another" (5:13). He expands the idea in Philippians when he writes:

> Do nothing from selfish ambition or conceit, but in humility count others more significant than yourselves. Let each of you look not only to his own interests, but also to the interests of others. Have this mind among yourselves, which is yours in Christ Jesus, who, though he was in the form of God, did not count equality with God a thing to be grasped, but emptied himself, by taking the form of a servant, being born in the likeness of men. (2:3-7)

There are a couple of things I want to point out in these verses. First, notice that he says we should look to the interests of others *in addition to our own*. It is easy when speaking of servanthood to sound like if you keep anything for yourself or do something for yourself at any time that you are selfish and making God angry, but this is not the case. Yes, it is important to serve others, but we must also take care of ourselves. It is impossible to serve others if we do not have the stamina, the resources, or just the plain desire to do so. We must feed and nourish ourselves physically, emotionally, intellectually, and spiritually so that we are able to help others do the same. Of course, we have to be careful of making this an excuse. "I have to eat this steak dinner so I can drop off a can of beans at the food shelf tomorrow" is not exactly the servant's heart that Jesus was teaching us about, nor is "I better take a nap this afternoon instead of doing the project my wife gave me so I have enough energy in case something bigger comes up tonight." But we do need to take care of ourselves, and Jesus showed us that as well. He would retreat by himself to pray or fast, returning after to continue serving and teaching others. Even the Lord God, who cannot tire, took a day off to rest after six days of creation. Many churches will offer their pastors sabbatical time for rest and rejuvenation. When the pastor returns, he is able to more fully care for and serve his congregation. Without any rest time, pastors can burn out and become overburdened, which does not serve their congregation very well at all. The same is true of ourselves. If we never allow ourselves time to sleep, eat a healthy meal, read the Bible, or any other number of things, we will become burned out and unable to properly serve our wives, families, churches, coworkers, or anyone else. Taking care of yourself is a good thing, but only if it then causes you to take care of others.

The second thing I want to point out about the verses in Philippians is that Paul equates our own servanthood to that of Jesus, and extols us to become like Christ in how we serve and care for others. This was also an important idea in the verses from Ephesians that we have already looked at, and this time Paul is speaking directly to how husbands treat their wives. "Husbands, love your wives, as Christ loved the church and gave himself up for her" (v. 25). Jesus is again our example, and He gave himself up for His bride (the church). In the same way, husbands ought to love their wives, care for them, consider them, put them first, and serve them.

It may seem like a contradiction to say that a husband must be his wife's quarterback and leader, and then say that he must serve her in any way he can, but it actually fits together perfectly. The greatest leaders serve their followers, and it is easy to see that example in Jesus. As we've already discussed, God became man to serve us, not to be served. Does that make God any less of our leader? Does it "bring Him down a notch" in our eyes? Of course not! He's still God, the creator of the universe! The fact that He came down to Earth as a man to serve us should actually make us want to follow Him even more. Tony Dungy enjoyed an amazing run of success as the head coach of the Indianapolis Colts, and in a piece he wrote for "Sharing the Victory" magazine, he said, "Ever since I've been in a leadership position, my focus has been the model of Christ as the servant-leader. There are different ways to lead, but I've always felt that it's better if other people follow me because they want to follow, not because I've been put up there as the leader and they have to follow. To do that, you have to earn people's trust and their respect; and the way to do that is to show them you are there to help them" (www.sharingthevictory.com). Dungy makes a very important point here. He wants people to follow him because they want to, not because they have to. He was speaking mainly as a football coach, but the same thing is true in our families. By serving our wives, it shows them how much we care about them and love them, and they want to follow us as their husbands, instead of begrudgingly following us because they think they have to. All the latter does is lead to frustration and anger on both sides. And when your wife is being served like that, it makes her want to serve you too. Showing love and care and consideration to her makes her want to show you those same things.

Now the question is, what does being a servant to your wife really look like? It's not a specific list of actions to take care of, and it is not a checklist of things that you can finish and then forget about. Rather, it's a mindset. It is always thinking, "What could I do to help her right now?" and "What would make her happy in this situation?" Sometimes it's easy to figure out because it's so obvious nobody could miss it, or because she specifically asks you to do something. But while it may be easy, that doesn't mean it's unimportant. If she has a bad day and now she's exhausted and she asks if it's okay to just order pizza for dinner, the servant husband says yes and orders the pizza himself, even if he doesn't feel much like pizza and was really hoping to have a nice home-cooked meal that night. Or she may ask him to watch the kids for a little while so she can relax in a warm bath, which the servant husband does happily, even though the playoffs are on TV. When the husband so willingly serves the wife, it makes her feel cared for, and she in turn wants to serve her husband as well, and perhaps waits until after the playoff game to have her warm bath. Then both husband and wife are lovingly considering each other, and are becoming a picture of Christ and His church.

The not-as-obvious moments to serve your wife come when she doesn't ask you to do anything, and perhaps does not even feel like she needs to be served at all. That is when the servant husband really shows her that he is constantly considering her. Clean the kitchen when she's out with the kids, or surprise her with a weekend away, or put the laundry in the dryer when you notice the washing machine is done, or any number of little things that really do make our wives feel like we are not just caring for them when we need to look good, but all of the time. One of my favorite things to do is during winter, when my wife is frantically trying to get out the door to go somewhere. I know what time she has to leave, so I take her keys and start the car so the windows are defrosted and the cab is warm when she wants to leave. It's a small thing, it takes all of 15 seconds, but it lets her know that I'm thinking about her and want her to be comfortable.

One last thing I want to say about serving your wife is that you may not always do it right. But usually, as long as you make an honest effort, she will still appreciate that you tried. I distinctly remember one day, early in our marriage, when my wife asked me to pick up some baking powder on my way home. No problem, I said. I went to the grocery store, looked around and found...baking soda. I knew I was looking for baking powder, but I didn't see anything labeled like that. So I wondered, "Is it the same thing?.....I don't see anything called baking powder.......They're probably the same thing." So I bought the baking soda and went home. Turns out, baking powder and baking soda are two very different things, which I learned when I got home. I tried to serve her, and I messed up. When that happens, first try to fix it if at all possible (I returned to the store and eventually found the baking powder), and second, try not to make that mistake again. Ever since that day, I have not mixed up baking powder and baking soda.

Lorenzo Neal is considered one of the best to ever play the game of football, but he built that reputation not on gaudy stats or self-serving play, but rather by making the players around him better and focusing on their success instead of his own. By doing the same with our wives, we can build a family environment that is loving, caring, and centered on others, just like Jesus did during His time here on Earth.

As Your Wife's Backup Quarterback...
You Need to be Her Encourager.

Backup quarterback is an extremely important position on a football team. It may seem like all they do is stand on the sidelines watching, but outside of the coaches, the backup quarterback is probably the most important person on the team who is likely to never step on the field. He may help read defenses, signal plays, tell the quarterback what to look for, give extra work to other players during practice, or even handle holding duties on kicks. But probably the most important thing he does is encourage the starting quarterback. The backup is not there to steal anyone's job, and he doesn't wish evil on the starter so he can get into the game. He maintains a positive attitude while hoping someone else succeeds instead of him. He's ready to play if he needs to, but until he does, he will help the starter and the rest of the team get ready for and win the game, encouraging them to play their best. Men, as your wife's backup quarterback, you need to be her encourager.

It is not difficult to see why encouragement is important. It builds us up, keeps us going, and makes us feel like we can meet our goals. But encouragement doesn't start with people, it starts with God. Our first, and most important, encouragement should come from the Lord. He is not a God who gives us a command and leaves us to ourselves without another thought. He encourages us and pushes us in our walk with Him. When Jesus was brought a paralytic, He told the man, "Take heart, my son; your sins are forgiven" (Matthew 9:2). Jesus then heals the man to glorify God in front of the people, but his initial encouragement was not for the physical healing, it was for the fact that the man's sins were forgiven due to his faith. It is important to recognize that through everything in life, we can be encouraged by the fact that God is faithful to his promises and if we remain faithful to Him then we will be rewarded with eternal life. Paul uses this idea in 1 Thessalonians 4, when he is talking about Jesus' return: "Then we who are alive, who are left, will be caught up together with them in the clouds to meet the Lord in the air, and so we will always be with the Lord. Therefore encourage one another with these words" (vs. 17-18). Notice what Paul wants the members of the church to focus on: The impending return of Jesus and our eternal life with Him. We are to encourage each other first with the knowledge that our faith in Jesus will result, ultimately, in spending eternity in paradise. Of course, beyond that we can offer encouragements in other ways, but they are all secondary to the encouragement that we get knowing that Jesus has promised to return, and God always keeps his promises.

It is important to note that the encouragement of the Lord, while it can be brought to us by family, friends, pastors, books, and many other things, comes from His Word. There are many reasons to consistently read the Bible, like learning about how to live in a Godly way, staying away from sin, discerning if what you hear about God is true, and others. But one thing we can get from reading the Bible consistently is the encouragement of God himself. To have the Word of God in our hands, encouraging us to stay strong in our faith (1 Corinthians 16:13), love each other (John 13:34), tell others about the Gospel (Matthew 28), and so many other things, is a gift from the Lord. The very fact that we have the Bible should encourage us that God loves us and wants to be in relationship with us so that we may find salvation in Him.

And that's one of the main things that encouragement does for everyone. It helps us build relationships with other people. The Bible shows that clearly in 1 Samuel 23, when Jonathan encourages David, telling him, "Do not fear, for the hand of Saul my father shall not find you. You shall be king over Israel, and I shall be next to you. Saul my father also knows this" (v. 17). Jonathan and David built a lasting friendship, mainly through encouraging each other to continue trusting in the Lord. Even after David became king and Jonathan had died, David brought Jonathan's son, Mephibosheth, into his own house because of the relationship he had with Jonathan. We see the same thing in our own relationships. When someone encourages us, we know that they care about us and want us to do well, and believe that we can do well. Well if we feel that way when we hear encouragement from others, imagine how much better it is if we hear it from our own spouse! If being encouraged builds your relationship with friends, family, or co-workers, how much more can your marriage relationship be built up if you make a point of offering words of encouragement to your spouse?! If she knows that you think she is doing a good job, not only will she keep doing it, but she will try to do it even more, and your relationship will be strengthened by your encouragement. But encouragement does not just show the other person that we think they can do well, it shows them that we actually want them to succeed.

In a culture like ours, we are taught at an early age to do everything we can to win. To hope somebody else succeeds, much less someone we're in direct competition with, is not in line with the "win at all costs" mentality that our society seems to have. But as a backup quarterback, we are actually encouraging someone else to succeed while that success means that we don't get in the game. Sometimes, though, we need to let our wives take initiative in certain things, and be there to encourage and help so that she can find success. Perhaps it is an event she's organizing, or a new plan she has to take care of the house, or a conversation she needs to have with a friend or family member. Whatever it is, it's important that our wives are encouraged to honor the Lord with what they do and feel like their husband supports them.

But this doesn't mean that we are supposed to be passive husbands, letting our wives take over our jobs. In fact, it means the complete opposite. We are actually leading our wives by encouraging them to get involved in the church, to bring the love of Christ to others, and to glorify God in the things she does. We are also maintaining our position of the leader by being ready to step in when needed. Sometimes, your wife may be struggling in her task. Whether it's a time crunch, or a difficult relationship, or a misunderstanding, or anything else, if your wife is struggling, you need to be ready to step in and take control so she can stop floundering. Eventually, she will be ready to step in once again with a new project or a new plan, and once again we need to be supportive and encouraging so she knows we want her to succeed, and that we believe she can. It's difficult to come back after a failure and try again, but it's easier if the person you love the most is telling you that they believe you can do it and they want you to succeed.

There is another time that the backup quarterback gets into the game, and that is when the quarterback has done such a great job that he no longer needs to play the rest of the game. This allows a few things for the starter. First, it allows the starter to rest. He has played hard most of the game, not to mention the week before the game, and now that the work has paid off and his team is way ahead, he has earned a chance to get a little rest. The backup gives him that by coming in and finishing out the game. The second thing is avoidance of injury. The starting quarterback is one of the most important players on the team, and an injury to him when he didn't need to be playing would devastate the team. So it allows him to guarantee that he's healthy for the next week's game and find success in his next task. Finally, it allows the quarterback to simply sit back and enjoy the victory. It's okay for us to enjoy it when things go well and when we perform well, as long as we remember that we can do nothing apart from God and all glory goes to Him, and so by finishing out the game after the outcome isn't in doubt allows the starter to enjoy the fact that he has had a great success.

All three of these things apply to our wives as well. As an example, say your wife has done a great job planning, organizing, and putting on a women's retreat at church. She spent months getting every detail into place, and the weekend went off without a hitch. God was glorified through her efforts, and the women of the church grew in their relationships with Him. So, after having this great success, maybe you step in to finish out the weekend. Allow her a chance to rest and thank the Lord for a wonderful weekend. So you take on the duties that she would normally do. You could take the kids out to an activity so she can rest at home, or you make dinner so she doesn't have to, or maybe you even take the family out to a restaurant to celebrate the great job that she did. Whatever it is, it allows her to rest after a success. The "avoidance of injury" parallel may seem hard to connect, but actually I think it's one of the easier connections to make. The difference is that in football the danger is in physical injury, while in our families the danger is in emotional injury. When our wives work so hard every day, with no chance to rest, it is easy for them to become burned out, frustrated, angry, disappointed, bitter, and many other negative things. If a football injury devastates the team, emotional injury can do much worse than that to a family and a marriage. We should not only be encouraging our wives to rest and relax every once in a while, but actively providing them an opportunity to do so.

The last point I want to make is that it doesn't take long to recognize why our wives need encouragement when we just look at the culture around us. We are consistently told that we are not good enough, whether it is through the media, from overbearing family members, from spiteful coworkers, or anything else. And the sad part is, we start to believe it. We believe that we are not good enough, not attractive enough, not smart enough, not strong enough, not happy enough, not rich enough, and not successful enough, but we can be if we would only do what that person/commercial/movie/book is telling us to do. But these are lies, pure and simple. We will never meet our expectations through anything in this world because this world is temporary and unfulfilling. It is only through Jesus that we can be truly happy with who we are. We are all made in the image of God, and if we accept that we can stop trying to find fulfillment in other things. This is, of course, not to say that we are perfect or we shouldn't try to improve ourselves. We should always be trying to improve ourselves, but the difference is that we need to do it for the glory of God and recognize the areas in our lives where we need to improve and the areas in which we need to be content with what God has given us.

Women feel these pressures more than anyone, and our wives are no exception. They are constantly told that if only they got this product, or wore this makeup, or dressed like this, or acted this way that they will be happier, healthier, and more desirable. The implication is that they are none of these things in their current state, and that is exactly why the encouragement of their husband is so important. We need to offset the negative messages of our culture and make sure that our wives know that we think they are intelligent, beautiful, hard working, nurturing, and important to us. Our wives should know that we do not view them the same way that society does, and we are not trying to manipulate them into thinking negatively about themselves for our own gain.

This encouragement of your wife is not, however, only done directly to your wife. What would happen if a backup quarterback started talking to his teammates and the media about how bad the starter was, how he can't win, and how the backup could do so much better? Nobody would take him seriously and he would create a negative feeling around the team. By taking shots at the starter, he is showing that he is selfish and arrogant instead of team-oriented and blessed.

As a married man, you will find yourself in positions and conversations focused on denigrating women, especially wives. The old "ball and chain" joke makes multiple appearances as we try to prove to each other who has the most demanding, nagging, no-fun wife. I have never really understood that, and I don't think I ever will. Why would I ever make public my wife's deficiencies and try to show other men that I am in a worse marriage than they are? Staying out of those conversations, or even responding with, "I guess I don't know, my wife is a really good cook" or something like that would go a long way to not only showing your wife how much you care about her and appreciate her, but also showing others that a wife is a person to be cherished and respected, not scorned and ridiculed.

It may not seem very exciting to be standing on the sideline rooting for somebody else to succeed, but it is a vital role, both on the team and in the family. Don't be a backup quarterback who pouts and hopes something happens to the starter so you can get in the game. Be the backup quarterback who encourages the starter to succeed, who is ready to come into the game to help out, and who does not speak poorly about the starter around others. Be an encourager instead of a discourager.

As Your Wife's Wide Receiver... You Need to Make the Big Plays.

During the course of a normal football game, the running back will take the ball 20-30 times and grind away each play for as many yards as he can get. During the 2013 NFL season, the running back with the best average yards per carry, Andre Ellington of the Arizona Cardinals, still averaged only 5.5 yards and carried the ball 118 times. An average rushing play in the NFL gains about three yards. There were only six players during the 2013 season that had a rushing play of over 70 yards, with the longest being 93 yards (and that play was actually by a quarterback, Terrelle Pryor of the Oakland Raiders). So the running backs have a difficult job because they have to take their short plays over and over, slowly and methodically moving the ball up the field. Sometimes, they may be able to break a long one, but it's pretty rare. In contrast, the wide receivers are the "skill position" players who touch the ball the least. Kenny Stills of the New Orleans Saints led the

NFL in average yards per catch in 2013 with 20.0, almost four times Ellington's rushing average, but Stills caught the ball only 32 times, only about a fourth of Ellington's touches. In fact, 150 receivers had a better yards-per-touch average than Andre Ellington, and 32 players in the league had a catch for at least 70 yards. So what does this tell us? That wide receivers make the big plays. They may not touch the ball nearly as often, but when they do, chances are a big gain is coming. While the running back does a really important, necessary job, it's just not that exciting to watch a guy take the ball and run three yards into a pile of people before he gets knocked to the ground. The excitement comes as the quarterback heaves the ball through the air for a receiver streaking toward the other team's end zone, and the moment that he catches the ball the crowd goes nuts as he turns on the jets in the open field. It may not happen very often, but when it does, it gets the fans standing and cheering and loving every second of it. Men, as your wife's wide receiver, you need to make the big plays.

When do these big plays need to take place? Not every day, not every week, and not even every month. If something special happens too often, then it becomes no longer special. If you bring your wife flowers every day, while she may appreciate it and enjoy it, by definition it is no longer special. Special is how we describe something that is out of the ordinary or doesn't happen very often. Even if you love a particular restaurant, if you eat there every single day, eventually you're going to get tired of it and want something else. Then, after a while, you go back to enjoy it again, and once again it is special.

This shouldn't be a new or surprising concept because in the church and even in our society we already do this. Certain days or events are given special importance, and we commemorate them as special. As a country, one of our biggest holidays is the 4th of July. It is a celebration of something that happened centuries ago, yet every year we gather with family and friends, grill dinner, and when the sun has set we shoot exploding devices into the sky with songs like "Born in the U.S.A." and "Proud to be an American" playing in the background. People dress in red, white, and blue, and we teach our kids that we live in a free country because a group of people in 1776 decided they weren't going to take it anymore, and since then millions of men and women have stood up for our right to freedom, and the 4th of July is our chance to celebrate that and thank the people who have made it possible. Similar celebrations occur on New Year's Day, Thanksgiving, Mothers' and Fathers' Day, and Halloween. These special events occur on local levels as well. One of my favorite events every August is the Minnesota State Fair. I look forward to it all summer, and I love going through all the buildings, seeing all the displays, and eating approximately 72 food items that come on a stick (and mini-donuts). It's a special tradition, and we all have them.

In the church, we mark special occasions as well. Christmas, Good Friday and Easter are obviously the big ones, but there are also days like Ash Wednesday or All Saints' Day that some churches like to celebrate. We give gifts, eat, get together with our families and friends, remember past celebrations, eat, marvel at how big the kids have gotten, and eat. And these days are special to us for a variety of reasons, but mostly because they mark something special that we don't want to lose the importance of or forget. Jesus' birth and death are two extremely important events, and we never want to forget their significance or lose it to gift buying and Hollidazzle parades.

The Bible itself even talks about special days and commemorating events. Obviously the Lord set apart the Sabbath Day as holy, but in addition to that He gave Israel various special days and celebrations so they could remember their past and keep connected to the things that God had done for them. In Exodus 12, as the Lord institutes the

Passover, He tells His people, "This day shall be for you a memorial day, and you shall keep it as a feast to the LORD; throughout your generations, as a statute forever...for on this very day I brought your hosts out of the land of Egypt" (vs. 14, 17). Not only does God give the day to the current generation, but throughout all the generations, forever. God knew how important it was for the Israelites to remember and commemorate their coming out of the land of Egypt. Not only did it keep all of the generations connected to their ancestry and help them remember what God had done for them in the past, but it became an important metaphor for what would come years later: The death of Jesus as the final sacrifice, the perfect Passover lamb (1 Corinthians 5:7). Had the Israelites forgotten about this event or not given it its proper importance, the early church would not have had an easy time drawing connections between what God did in the past and what He was doing among them at the time. Similarly, God institutes the Day of Atonement in Leviticus 16, and then in Leviticus 23 gives the nation the Feast of Firstfruits, the Feast of Weeks, the Feast of Trumpets, and the Feasts of Booths. All of these celebrations were intended to help the people remember and celebrate what God had done for them and their ancestors, in addition to pointing to Jesus' death and resurrection. He labeled these days as special and the community treated them that way.

And yet, with all of those days already made important by God or by culture, we joke about how a husband cannot remember his wife's birthday. We laugh with each other about how we remember the date that the U.S. beat the Soviet Union in the 1980 Olympics, but struggle to recall our anniversary. This is a problem that needs rectifying. If, as we claim, our wives are the most important people in our lives, then the first dates that we should be able to recall are her birthday, anniversary, or any other day deemed special by the two of you. Maybe the day you met has special significance, or the day you went on your first date, or the day you proposed. Whatever the case, these are special days that are important to commemorate. The day you get married is, hopefully, one of the best days of your life. It signals your joining together in Christ, starting your new life together, and acts as a public statement that you are entering into a covenant relationship that you will not break. Does that sound like a day that is best commemorated by a 99-cent Hallmark card? I hope not! The day your wife was born is the day that God sent her into this world and started preparing her for your relationship. Does that sound like a day that is best recognized with dinner at the McDonald's down the block? No! These are special occasions that deserve special recognition.

The word "special" is the key here. Do something out of the ordinary, something unexpected, and something that you know she will like. That's another key point. Since you're doing it for her, it should be special for her. Hopefully you know your wife well enough that you can come up with something that she will love. Don't do something that you would enjoy, and don't take somebody else's idea, really figure out something that is for her. Getting tickets to an NFL game may work if she loves football and hasn't been to a game in years, but it doesn't work if she's not big on football, no matter how much you would enjoy going to the game. Along the same lines, let's say that you're driving down the road and she remarks that she would love to try a fancy restaurant as you go by. You file that away, and a few months later surprise her with birthday reservations for that restaurant. She's surprised, excited, and impressed that you listened to her. You go and have a wonderful time, so when your anniversary rolls around you make reservations there again. Again, she's excited, but it's no longer totally new. At the same restaurant for Valentine's Day, she still has a good time, but it's starting to feel routine. After four years of every possible special occasion being celebrated at that restaurant, she's wondering if she'll ever get to eat anywhere else. You think you're doing a great job bringing her to this fancy restaurant for special occasions, and she certainly does appreciate it, but it's no longer special because it's not out of the ordinary or unexpected.

See, the main reason that we do special things to recognize special days is to show our wives how special they are to us. And if we fall into a rut of just doing the same things over and over, or not doing them at all, our wives will not feel special. By doing the special things, we are showing them how much we care about them, how happy we want to make them, and how special those days are to us too.

I want to go back to the idea that the key is the word "special." Notice that the key word is not "expensive" or "extravagant" or anything like that. It's difficult for some guys to get rid of the idea that anything special has to be expensive. Sometimes you'll do something that costs a good amount of money as something special, but it's not the money that makes it special, it's the time you put into it, the details you've coordinated, and just simply the fact that you love your wife so much that you want to do something for her. Some of the best things Lindsey and I have done for each other didn't cost much at all. Our first Valentine's Day together, six weeks after we started dating, I went to visit her at college and arrived with a giant pink bag that included about 60 individually wrapped gifts. That sounds like a lot, but not when you know that every gift was a cheap little thing with hearts on it from the party store. Cups, candies, headbands, necklaces, rings, and a multitude of other red, plastic items were part of the bounty, each one costing between 25 cents and a dollar. She loved it, her roommates loved it, and luckily I had a roommate who would help me wrap all that stuff. When we got married, she contacted a huge list of my friends and family asking them to write a short paragraph about my relationship with them and what I mean to them. Then she collected them all in a book and gave it to me the day before our wedding. I still have that book and still page through it, reading the notes from people I love and who love me. It was an amazing, special, not-expensive gift that I will cherish forever. Neither one of these things cost a lot of money, but they were special and unforgettable.

I did a lot of other things for Lindsey's birthday and other special days when we were dating, and she always loved it and felt so wonderful that I would do those things for her. But there is also a caution there: I did those things while we were dating. When I first came up with all of the positions I am writing about in this book, I asked Lindsey to rank me 1-10 on each one so that I would know where I was doing well and where I needed work. To my surprise, the lowest score she gave me was on Wide Receiver. As we are prone to do, I objected to save face. "But I've done a lot of that!"

"Yes," she answered, "You did a lot of that when we were dating, but not really since we've been married." And she was absolutely right. I hadn't thought much about it, but she noticed my lack of attention to this area. This happens to a lot of guys, I think, and not just out of laziness. Things change after we're married. Finances get tighter, children are born, we have a career, and so the time and money we used to be able to dedicate to these special events doesn't seem to be as readily available anymore. But let's be honest. Some of it *is* laziness. We tend to do everything we can to get the girl to marry us, and then once she does we figure she's locked in and we don't have to try as hard anymore. But in truth, we should be trying harder. We should be giving even more effort to show her that she married a man who loves her and cherishes her and wants to do something special for her. So I apologized and told her I would try to do better.

The next year was our 5th anniversary, so I decided to do something really special. And what was my first thought? If it's special, it has to be expensive! So I started looking at lodges on the north shore of Lake Superior where we had honeymooned. Then I looked at our bank account. Then I decided maybe we could just stay at a hotel in Minneapolis and do fun things around the Twin Cities. Then I looked at our bank account. So I thought maybe we could just stay at home and do fun things around the Twin Cities. Fun, free things. I was disappointed at first, but I reminded myself that Lindsey was not going to be concerned with how much I had spent, she was just going to be appreciative that I had put all this together. So that weekend, we sent the kids off to my mom's house and spent four days together walking around lakes, grilling dinner, watching movies, and just generally reinvigorating our marriage. It was wonderful, it was inexpensive, and it was special. I also tried to incorporate things from our history together. We went out for cheesecake because we had cheesecake at our wedding. We got pizza and watched a Twins game because we did that one night on our honeymoon. The night of our actual anniversary, we got out the unity candle from our wedding and lit it together. We've done this every year since we got married. It's not a big thing, but it helps us remember that we are one in Christ and that on August 20, 2005, we made a promise to each other to be together forever. To Lindsey, it's a special tradition, so I made sure to remember to incorporate that into our weekend. We had a great time and I look forward to the next time I get to plan a special celebration for her.

When will that special celebration be, though? Well, obviously her birthday or Valentine's Day are prime candidates, but she knows when those happen. There's no element of surprise as far as the day goes. That brings us to the most special celebration of all: the one she doesn't even know is coming. Nothing surprises her more than celebrating a day she didn't even know was worth celebrating. Maybe you happen to remember the date that you first told her you love her. Or maybe it's the day you bought your first house. Or maybe you're coming up on 5,000 days married to each other. Whatever it is, surprising her with a special event on a day she didn't remember will not only excite her, it will show her that you are in tune with your relationship and that the important events from your history are still important to you today. She doesn't have to see you like the buffoon husband on so many TV shows who can't remember his wife's middle name. She can see you as the man who loves her and wants to show her how special she is.

So make the big play. It may not happen very often, but when it does, grab that long pass in the open field and turn on the jets. It will be exciting, it will be special, and it will remind her of the "big plays" that Christ has made for his church.

As Your Wife's Special Teams...
You Need to be Her Clutch Performer.

There is a moment, during most football games, when a big play is needed. But not just a big play. A huge play. A clutch play. Big plays are fun and can happen at any moment. They rev up the team and the fans cheer for them. But a clutch play? A clutch play is different. Clutch plays happen in that moment where success can mean victory and failure can mean defeat. It may be at the end of the game when the team has one last chance to win, or it may come at a time when one more score by the opponent will put the game out of reach, or perhaps at a moment when the team is so downtrodden that they need a bolt of energy to rouse them and spur them toward victory when it seems there is no hope. In any of these cases, the clutch play does not usually come from the usual players who are out there all game. It comes from a group that is sometimes forgotten, sometimes dismissed, and sometimes even mocked. It is the Special Teams. Their name should tell you enough about what they do. This is not a normal group of men who play a certain position and are celebrated for their excellence. This is a special group. This group does not concern itself with playing time, accolades, or huge salaries. They do whatever is needed to help the team, and in that clutch moment they are the ones to take the field and come through when the team needs it most. They score game-winning field goals, block punts, return kickoffs, and do whatever is asked of them, and in the end their clutch play brought the team to victory. Men, as your wife's Special Teams, you need to be her Clutch Performer.

One play that can be clutch is bringing back a kick for a touchdown. If it is a kickoff, the other team has just scored, and no doubt the team is disappointed or a little deflated. But when the return man breaks free and races down the field, the team is once again cheering and getting excited, and the score is back to where it was before the opponents' touchdown or field goal. If it is a punt, the team is feeling good about how they stopped their opponent, and a punt return for a score excites everyone even more and makes the other team feel like the game is getting out of reach. The best in NFL history at bringing kicks back all the way is Devin Hester of the Chicago Bears, who has scored 17 touchdowns off of kickoff or punt returns during his career, and also returned a kickoff in a Super Bowl. Of those returns, nine have either tied the score or given the Bears the lead, three of them provided the eventual game-winning points, and seven of them have come in the fourth quarter. In 2006, Hester brought a punt back 83 yards to the end zone against the Arizona Cardinals on Monday Night Football, giving the Bears a 24-23 comeback victory. That's clutch.

But perhaps the most common clutch play in football is the game-winning field goal as time expires. At that moment, the field goal unit comes onto the field knowing that their team's victory or defeat depends on them. Some of them may not have stepped onto the field at all during the game, but at this moment, with everything on the line, they are ready to perform. One of the most clutch kickers in history is Adam Vinatieri. While with the New England Patriots during the 2001 playoffs, Vinatieri kicked a 45-yard field goal as time expired to send the game to overtime...in near-blizzard conditions. He then won the game with a 23-yarder in overtime, and a few weeks later won the Super Bowl with a 48-yard field goal on the final play of the game. Two years later, he again booted the Patriots to a championship with a 41-yard field goal with four seconds remaining in the game. He is the only player in history to be the deciding factor in two Super Bowl wins. That's clutch.

The Bible gives us many great examples of men in history who were absolutely clutch, but when I think of a clutch performer, two men pop into my mind first. The first is one of the most famous men in the Bible in one of the most famous stories. The book of 1 Samuel tells about the Israelite army camped in the desert, cowering and hiding in fear of the Philistines' main weapon: Goliath. For 40 days, Goliath, standing over nine feet tall, would come out and challenge the Israelites to send out their best warrior to fight, one-on-one. The loser's nation would become slaves to the winner's nation. Well, nobody in the Israelite army wanted to face the guaranteed defeat that was Goliath. Except David. David, the young sheepherder who had been anointed the next king of Israel, saw no compelling reason that he shouldn't go out there and fight Goliath, so he volunteered. When asked what he would need for this moment that was one of the biggest in the nation's history, that could decide the fate of Israel for the foreseeable future, David responded that he didn't need anything. No armor, no big weapons, just the knowledge that he was battling on behalf of the true Lord God. So at this definitive moment in Israel's history, David took his sling and five stones he found by the river, and faced Goliath in battle. The Philistines laughed at him...until David defeated Goliath with one shot.

The young shepherd, who was not a warrior or experienced in fighting or intimidating in stature, trusted the Lord and stepped up when his people needed him the most, and defeated the seemingly-invincible Goliath. That's clutch.

The other example the Bible gives us is the leader of the early church, Peter. Acts 2 tells the story of the Day of Pentecost after Jesus rose from the dead and ascended back to Heaven, promising that He would send the Holy Spirit to them. Sure enough, on that day, as the disciples gathered in the Upper Room, the Spirit descended upon them. As a result, many of the disciples began speaking in different languages, and the people in the city who heard them were amazed that everyone seemed to hear the disciples speaking in their own language. There was a lot of confusion and questions about how these men were able to do this, and some even suggested that the men were just drunk and their slurs sounded like an actual language.

That day may have decided the path of the early church and the gospel of Jesus. If nobody would have spoken up, explained to the people what was happening, or given any context of the faith they would be telling them about in the coming days, weeks, and months, they may very well have been thought of as fools or some weird cult that drinks too much and can't pronounce words properly. But Peter, who was already known as being part of Jesus' inner circle of friends, stood up and gave a sermon to everyone who would listen, proclaiming the miracle of Jesus' death and resurrection and exhorting the people to believe in Jesus as the Messiah and place their faith in Him. It was a moment of decision, a moment when somebody had to step up as a leader and take charge of the situation, and a moment of extreme gravity in the life of the early church. Either they would become a legitimate movement that people would believe in or they would fade away into nothing and be completely forgotten. Peter took charge. He stood up and delivered the sermon that is recorded in Acts 2:14-36, and three thousand people were added to their number on that one day. The message of Jesus could have faded into oblivion, but instead thousands of people came to believe in Jesus because of Peter's impromptu sermon in the city. That's clutch.

As husbands, we need to be just as clutch for our wives. We need to come through when our wives need us the most. But what does that look like? For one thing, while it may seem similar to some positions we've already talked about, like Running Back or Wide Receiver, there are important differences. The "Worker" aspect of Running Back is a consistent, everyday effort at providing for the family in various ways. The "Big Playmaker" aspect of Wide Receiver is driven by you and your desire to show her she's special and celebrate significant days. But the "Clutch Performer" aspect of Special Teams only comes up once in a while, so it's not a daily thing, and it's not driven by you, it's driven by your wife. Anniversary dinners are planned by you and you know they're coming long in advance. Clutch situations come from your wife and they spring up out of nowhere.

Of course, how it comes up and what she needs largely depends on the situation. Maybe she had a hard day and is ready to pull her hair out so you arrange for a babysitter and take her out to dinner to regain her sanity. Or maybe she's making dinner for a party and realizes she's missing one ingredient, and she can't leave but without that ingredient her whole dish doesn't work and she doesn't have anything else to serve so she calls you and says you have to drive back to the special grocery store 10 miles in the opposite direction to get that ingredient because she has to have it to make the dish and SHE IS NOT GOING TO THE PARTY WITH NOTHING TO SERVE! So you turn around, even though you're almost home, and go get that ingredient for her. It doesn't seem like a big deal to you, but it's important to her, and you just came through in the clutch. It's important to remember that just because a situation may not feel clutch to you, it still could to her, and she's the one who needs you to come through.

One of the reasons it is important to come through for your wife in those clutch situations is because it shows her that she gets priority in your life. She gets placed ahead of work, friends, games, and anything else that could impede the husband's ability to put her first. Instead of doing what is most convenient for yourself, do what helps her when she's in a tough spot and show her that she is your #1 priority. Now, understand that I don't mean she gets to dictate everything you do, and common sense needs to come into play. If she asks you to leave work to do something for her that is not especially urgent and you know you'll get in trouble with your boss for that, explain to her that it is not possible this time. But be careful not to use that as an excuse to never come through for her when she needs it the most.

Whatever the situation is, coming through when she needs it the most will help your wife trust you and have confidence in you. If you want to be a leader of your family, then you have to come through when it's most important. People naturally look up to those who perform when the pressure is on, and those people become leaders. If your wife knows that she can trust you and she has confidence in you, she will be more willing to follow you as the leader of the family.

Another thing to keep in mind is that the players who come through in the clutch do not let failure affect them the next time they are called onto the field. Adam Vinatieri has missed plenty of kicks in his life, a few of them probably at the end of the game with a chance to win. But when he came out during the Super Bowl with a chance to win the game, did he think to himself, "Oh no, I've missed kicks before. I may miss this one too. I should just tell Coach that I don't even want to try so I don't fail again"? Of course not. He went onto the field when his team needed him the most and won the championship. At that moment, he didn't care that he had missed in the past. It was about that game, that moment, that kick, and he was going to do it for his team. We may not always come through for our wives perfectly, but don't let that affect how hard you work at it the next time.

Don't dwell on your failures of the past, focus on succeeding in the present. It is that day, that moment, that your wife needs you, and you need to come through for her when she needs it the most. That's clutch.

As Your Wife's Offensive Lineman... You Need to be Her Protector.

One of the most exciting plays in football is the big hit. Despite the growing awareness of the severity of concussions and the movements at every level to make the game safer, fans still clamor for the big hit. We cheer our team when they make the hit, then watch the replay in slow motion, then watch it again online, then send the link to our friends so they can watch it online, and on and on. We love big hits... except against our players. We don't want our players to get hit like that, because it could mean an injury. We want to see penalty flags thrown on the other team. We cry foul if it's a late hit. And the player we want to see getting hit the least is our quarterback. The quarterback is the leader of the team, and probably the most important player on the field. So what do we do? We put five or six large men in front of the quarterback so nobody will hit him. We protect that most important player on the team. It is no coincidence that teams with great quarterbacks have great offensive lines. When the quarterback has no worries about getting hit or running away from people, it's much easier for him to settle down and do his job. If he's constantly worried about what may befall him, he gets jittery, makes bad passes, throws interceptions, and doesn't do his job very well. Protection is key to success.

One of the most famous examples that show the importance of protecting the quarterback happened on November 18, 1985. On that day, Joe Theismann, quarterback of the Washington Redskins, suffered a career-ending leg injury as he was sacked by Lawrence Taylor of the New York Giants. The video of that play has been shown countless times, and stands as the example of why protection is so important. Men, as your wife's offensive lineman, you need to be her protector.

The main thing I want to address in this chapter is protecting your wife physically, not spiritually or emotionally. That's a topic for a whole different chapter. And let's clarify that "physical protection" does not always mean "physical strength." When I say "physical" I basically mean "tangible." Tangible, concrete ways that you can protect your wife and keep her safe. God takes care of us that way, and we need to take care of our wives that way. While much of our idea of God's protection revolves around the spiritual, the Bible makes it plain that He will also protect us physically. It starts in the first chapter of Genesis, when God tells Adam and Eve, "Behold, I have given you every plant yielding seed that is on the face of all the earth, and every tree with seed in its fruit. You shall have them for food" (v. 29). Sin has not entered the world yet, but God is protecting Adam and Eve by providing for their physical needs, and that physical protection continues throughout the Bible:

-Sparing Noah and his family from the flood (Genesis 6-7)

-Protecting and guiding the Israelites as a pillar of smoke or fire (Exodus 13)

-Giving the Israelites passage through the Red Sea (Exodus 14)

-Sending manna and quail to the Israelites in the desert (Exodus 16)

-Giving the Israelites victory in battle (Joshua 11-12, among many others)

-Providing for Ruth and Naomi after their husbands have died (Ruth 1-4)

-Saving David from Goliath (1 Samuel 17) and from the hand of King Saul (1 Samuel 19, among others)

-Restoring Job after all of his loss (Job 42)

-Keeping Shadrach, Meshach, and Abednego safe in the fiery furnace (Daniel 3)

-Keeping Daniel safe in the lions' den (Daniel 6)

-Feeding over 5,000 people with five loaves of bread and two fish (John 6)

-Calming a terrible storm while at sea (Mark 4)

-Saving Paul and everyone else during a shipwreck (Acts 27)

On a broader scale, many of these passages and stories point to Jesus in the New Testament, but in the specific context of the story you can see that there are many examples of God protecting His people, and this isn't even a complete list. The people understood that God would protect them and wrote about it a lot, praising Him and thanking Him for doing so. The Psalms are a common place that God is praised for His protection with verses like these:

-In peace I will both lie down and sleep; for you alone, O LORD, make me dwell in safety. (4:8)

-The LORD is my rock and my fortress and my deliverer, my God, my rock, in whom I take refuge, my shield, and the horn of my salvation, my stronghold. (18:2)

-The angel of the LORD encamps around those who fear him, and delivers them. (34:7)

-God is our refuge and strength, a very present help in trouble. Therefore we will not fear though the earth gives way, though the mountains be moved into the heart of the sea, though its waters roar and foam, though the mountains tremble at its swelling. (46:1-3)

-The LORD is your keeper; the LORD is your shade on your right hand. The sun shall not strike you by day, nor the moon by night. The LORD will keep you from all evil; he will keep your life. The LORD will keep your going out and your coming in from this time forth and forevermore. (121:5-8)

Obviously, many, if not all, of these verses can be taken as talking about God's spiritual protection of his people, and they certainly do, but they also imply a sort of physical protection from God. The images of the sun and the moon, the encampment, the waves and the mountains, are all images that show God's protection of us in a physical, concrete way. In fact, God is referred to as a "fortress" over a dozen times throughout the Old Testament. What is the point of a fortress? To protect the inhabitants from outsiders. There is no way a man can ward off an army standing in an open field, so he retreats to his fortress, where he can be protected. If we are in relationship with the Lord, we can be confident that we can take refuge in Him as our fortress and be protected.

But how does this sort of protection translate to our role as husbands? Well, just like the Bible gives us examples of God's protection, it also gives us examples of men protecting each other, and especially their wives and children. In Numbers 1, the Lord told Moses, "Take a census of all the congregation of the people of Israel, by clans, by fathers' houses, according to the number of names, every male, head by head. From twenty years old and upward, all in Israel who are able to go to war..." (vs. 2-3). In order to know how many people were able to go to war, Moses had to count all the *men*. Going to war was not something that women were expected to do, and that sort of protection was something the men of Israel were expected to provide. Of course, this is a very broad example, but Peter gets much more specific to husbands in 1 Peter 3:7 saying, "Likewise, husbands, live with your wives in an understanding way, showing honor to the woman as the weaker vessel, since they are heirs with you of the grace of life." This is a verse that has been the topic of much discussion since the term "weaker vessel" seems to have a negative connotation, but it really doesn't. Peter is speaking specifically to a husband and a wife, not to men and women in general. So a man should marry a woman that he will be able to honor and protect, and a woman should marry a man that she knows will be able to protect her. Again, that does not mean marrying a man who is physically stronger than she is, but a man who is willing to keep her safe and recognize ways that he can keep her away from danger. Protecting his wife is a responsibility given to each husband, and he should not take it lightly.

But what does that protection look like in our culture and how the world is now? I'm willing to bet that not many men need to protect their wives from bands of marauders or opposing armies in their backyards, but that doesn't mean that just because those types of things don't exist or are not close to us that we don't need to protect our wives. One of the main ways we can protect our wives is by giving them a safe place to live. Sometimes this is easier said than done, and often there is little we can control about our surrounding community, but when you are choosing where to live, the safety of the area should play a large role so neither of you has to worry when she is home alone or out walking by herself or something like that. And if the area becomes unsafe and moving is not an option, you need to do what you can to increase the safety of your own home. Maybe new deadbolts on the doors, or an alarm system for the house, or a large dog. All of these are possible ways that you can protect your wife and keep her safe. Protecting her by keeping her safe also means looking for ways she could get hurt and fixing them. In the winter, I always keep our driveway and sidewalk shoveled and salted so that neither my wife nor the kids will fall on the ice. It sounds minor, but I know multiple people who have had some pretty bad injuries just by slipping on ice, so I want to do what I can to prevent that from happening to her. Maybe where you live, it's not ice, it's heat. Are you doing what you can to provide relief from it? Or maybe there's a broken stair in your house that somebody could trip on.

Did you fix it? Maybe the car she drives needs an oil change. Did you take care of that? There are many practical ways that you can protect your wife and keep her safe, and it is up to you to recognize those things before she gets hurt, rather than after.

Another way to protect our wives in our society is to keep them out of situations that could result in harm, no matter how unlikely. If someone knocks on the door and we're not expecting anyone, I answer the door, not her. The chances that it will end badly are extremely small, but they aren't zero, so I won't take the chance. I have the same philosophy about the popular website Craig's List, where people can sell or trade items. When she wants to buy something from somebody on Craig's List, I go to pick it up, not her. Again, the odds that danger is waiting on the other end is so small it's easy to not think about it. But I have to think about it, because that chance exists. So I always pick up what she needs, or if I can't, I insist that somebody go with her, whether her mom or her sister or a friend, but I feel better knowing that somebody else is there with her and she isn't alone. That's my job as her husband, to protect her and keep her safe as much as I can.

An unfortunate feeling in our current culture is that when there is talk of husbands protecting their wives, a lot of people think that the implication is that women cannot take care of themselves. Like if we try to protect our wives, we are saying they are incapable and weak. But this is obviously not the reason we take our wives' protection seriously. If your wife believes that you are being condescending by trying to protect her, a frank discussion should be had between the two of you so that you both understand that it is not her limitations that drive you to protect her, but rather your loving concern for her. And this will also come out of the way you treat her every day. If she feels disrespected and patronized on a regular basis, she will feel the same when you try to take care of her, but if she feels loved and respected every day, she will understand that your protection is not due to her own inadequacy, but due to the fact that she has a husband who wants to take care of her and keep her safe.

I should add one thing to this discussion, and it is that you can't protect her all of the time from everything. Of course you do your best and everything you can, but sometimes things happen that we cannot prevent. Just like we know that God can always protect us, but sometimes does not, for reasons we may know or not know, we know that everything we do to protect our wives is helpful, but not exhaustive. Even though we dig in at the line scrimmage, ready to protect, sometimes the quarterback gets sacked from the other side. Or sometimes the defensive rush is just too much and we can't block everyone. That happens sometimes, but when it does, what does the line do? They line up again, ready to protect on the next play. When it doesn't work, we cannot sulk in failure. We have to line up and try again, ready to see the next way that our wife needs protection, and ready to do it.

As Your Wife's Defensive Back... You Need to be Her Guardian.

When the opposing team has the ball, everyone on the defense needs to be prepared to do their job and stop the ball. But obviously not everyone plays in the same spot. Generally, there are three levels of the defense: the defensive line, the linebackers, and the defensive backs. This has to give the defenders a certain amount of relief, knowing they're not the only ones trying to stop the ball. If the ball gets past the defensive line, they know the linebackers can take care of it. If it gets past the linebackers, they know the defensive backs will cover it. If it gets past the defensive backs....Huh. Well, if it gets past the defensive backs, it's a touchdown. Security is not there for the defensive backs. They are the last line of defense. If they don't stop the attack, nobody will. Men, as your wife's Defensive Back, you need to be her guardian.

Of course, in football, the quickest way to stop the other team's attack is to simply take the ball away from their offense. If they don't have the ball, they can't do any damage. The best at taking the ball away was Hall-of-Famer Paul Krause, who had 81 interceptions during 16 seasons with the Washington Redskins and Minnesota Vikings, an NFL record. When Jerry Burns introduced Krause at his Hall of Fame Induction Ceremony, Burns quoted legendary coach Bud Grant as saying, "Paul personified the term free safety. For 12 years, he was in a sense, free to play down and distance, the tendencies, quarterbacks' eyes, double key receivers, play a hunch, use his intelligence and great athletic ability to be one of the greatest free safeties that have ever played in the National Football League." Krause was his team's last line of defense, and they knew with him on the field they had a great chance of stopping the other team's attack.

As husbands, we are also the last, and most important, line of defense for our wives and families. If you don't think we are under attack, either you just don't know what you're looking for or you're oblivious to the attacks. Spiritual warfare was not created by old preachers to scare people into coming to church, no matter what our world would have you believe. Spiritual warfare is a reality, and it happens in our world every moment of every day. The Bible makes it plain throughout that the struggle between good and evil is not carried out with the friendliness of a rec league softball game; it is a fierce war that is waged with intensity and passion. The Bible refers to spiritual warfare as a battle (1 Samuel 17:47), the devil as the enemy (Matthew 13:39), the followers of Christ as soldiers (2 Timothy 2:3), and even uses the word "war" when describing the struggle we face with the devil (Luke 14:31, 1 Timothy 1:18, 2 Corinthians 10:3-5). This battle is not something that we can take lightly, so it is imperative that we guard our wives against attack from the enemy.

Just like a defensive back, the best way we can stop the enemy's attack is by intercepting it. If an offense doesn't have the ball, they can't score, and if the devil's attack doesn't get through, it can't affect your wife. To do this most effectively, you really have to be aware of what's going on in your wife's life and the things she's being influenced by. Be aware of what movies she's seeing, TV shows she's watching, websites she's reading, books she's discussing, people she's hanging out with, and advice she's hearing. All of those things can be entertaining, beneficial, and opportunities for growth, but they can also create subtle seeds of doubt, anger, or fear. It's important to know what and who is out there so you can offer suggestions that will move her to something God-honoring instead of God-defiling. Stop those negative influences from ever arriving, and they are not negative influences anymore. They are non-influences.

It is also true that sometimes the defensive back doesn't just intercept the ball, but even brings it all the way back the other way for a touchdown. This can happen with husbands and wives as well. Sometimes you may intercept an attack on your wife and guide her to something else that she likes even better. Or perhaps you shut down an attack from a TV show and replace it with encouraging words to her. Not only does this negate the enemy's attack, but it brings the situation completely in the other direction and makes your wife feel loved, honored, and cherished, which of course is always the goal.

In fact, sometimes the best defense is a good offense. In Ephesians 6, when Paul describes preparing for spiritual warfare, there is an element of attack in his description:

> Finally, be strong in the Lord and in the strength of his might. Put on the whole armor of God, that you may be able to stand against the schemes of the devil. For we do not wrestle against flesh and blood, but against the rulers, against the authorities, against the

cosmic powers over this present darkness, against the spiritual forces of evil in the heavenly places. Therefore take up the whole armor of God, that you may be able to withstand in the evil day, and having done all, to stand firm. Stand therefore, having fastened on the belt of truth, and having put on the breastplate of righteousness, and, as shoes for your feet, having put on the readiness given by the gospel of peace. In all circumstances take up the shield of faith, with which you can extinguish all the flaming darts of the evil one; and take the helmet of salvation, and the sword of the Spirit, which is the word of God, praying at all times in the Spirit, with all prayer and supplication. To that end keep alert with all perseverance, making supplication for all the saints, and also for me, that words may be given to me in opening my mouth boldly to proclaim the mystery of the gospel, for which I am an ambassador in chains, that I may declare it boldly, as I ought to speak. (vs. 10-20)

All of the things Paul talks about are things that we should make sure our wives are fitted with. They need to be surrounded by truth, not the lies of this world. They need to be covered in righteousness, protected by faith, sure of their salvation, and able to use the Word of God. And it can't be just every once in a while when it's convenient for you, it has to be all the time, like Paul says, "Keep alert with all perseverance."

If you are aware of what your wife needs, and you make sure she gets it, she will be less likely to meet those needs with any outside influences. If you tell her she's beautiful, and act like it, she won't seek approval of her looks from other people and she won't try to live up to our culture's standard of beauty. If you encourage her to read the Bible and other books that will help her grow, she won't use her time watching TV shows or reading websites that do little more than waste time. If you memorize scripture with her, she will have a base of Godly knowledge when making decisions and reacting to situations. If you make sure she can be part of a small group at church, she will have the support and suggestions of other Godly women, and will be able to support and advise them as well. All of these things will help you and your wife stop the attacks of the enemy.

Let's be clear, though, that all of those things that will help her cannot be forced on her if she's reluctant or apprehensive. You can't make her read the Bible, or memorize verses, or be part of a small group, or anything else. Instead, you have to teach her why all of those things are important and lovingly encourage her to get involved in them. And don't shove it all on to her at once, help her get comfortable and grow in the process. Maybe she starts by reading a few verses every day, and then moves to a chapter, and then a few chapters. Or maybe she goes to a small group a couple times, and then finds a group she wants to be in consistently, and then leads a women's group. It's all a process to be learned, not an ocean to dive into. It's also important that you remain a part of her growth. Talk to her about what she's reading, ask her how her small group went, memorize verses with her, and just generally let her know that you're not setting her off on a path and you hope it goes well, but that you're going to be walking alongside her. Having that support will help her continue on the path, and will hopefully make the attacks of the enemy less frequent.

One of the best ways to see who is a great defensive back is not always by tackles or passes defended, or even interceptions, but rather by noticing how often the opponent decides to *not* throw the ball in his direction. When the quarterback is making a split-second decision about where to throw the ball, he will likely decide to throw against the poorer defender. If one of the defensive backs is known as being great at stopping the offense, they're not going to throw the ball that way. So the stats may look average, but every opposing quarterback knows how great that defensive back is. In a 2009 NFL Films Documentary, Coach Bill Belichick and Quarterback Tom Brady of New England were shown preparing for a game against the Baltimore Ravens. When watching film of the Ravens, one question they asked on every play was, "Where's Ed?" Ed Reed, widely considered one of the best defensive backs in the league, is so good at what he does that opposing coaches and quarterbacks often don't even try to beat him, they just avoid him. When guarding our wives from attack, a similar idea applies. When we work hard at it and become good at it, the devil's attacks will not only be easier to defend, but less frequent all together.

Of course, no matter how good the defensive backs may be, inevitably the other team will score a touchdown eventually. Maybe they can shut out the offense for a quarter, or even a game, but for an entire season, or an entire career, success will not come 100% of the time. Eventually, an attack on your wife will get through. Someone may approach her with harsh words, or she may start feeling angry or frustrated in the home, or she goes to a friend's house where they suggest watching a movie that is clearly not God-honoring. Whatever the case, your wife will be attacked, and you can't protect her from everything all of the time. But in football, when the defensive back fails and the other team scores, do his teammates start complaining, "Oh, great! Now there's no way we can win the game! You've lost it for us and there's nothing we can do!"? No, they recognize the fact that the other team scored, and then begin preparing to fight back. They know that the game isn't over until the final buzzer sounds, and we know that the war we're fighting will go on until the Lord takes us home. So all of the things that you do to help guard your wife will prepare her for when an attack does get through. She won't simply wilt under the pressure and assume that all is lost, she'll see that the attack got through and she'll be prepared to fight against it. She'll respond lovingly to harsh criticism, she'll recall verses about being slow to anger, or she'll politely excuse herself from watching the movie with her friends. Whatever the attack is, she will be ready to recognize it and counter it because of the training she has been getting from God.

One important thing that every defense does is try to figure out how the other team scored. What happened that they were able to break down the wall and get an attack through? When they can figure that out, they can try to fix it. If our wives are subject to an attack, no matter how well or poorly they are able to respond, we should think about how that attack got through and then try to fix it. This can be very tricky because we can't cut ourselves off from the world, but we should think about if there's anything we can do to limit the attacks on our wives. Perhaps it is a matter of telling someone that in the future they can speak with you about any concerns they have instead of going directly to her. Maybe she needs to stop associating with certain people if their company leads her to sinful behavior. Or maybe it's just helping her get organized so that she's not prone to bursts of anger and frustration when things aren't going smoothly during the day. One thing my wife has struggled with is idleness on the computer. She felt like she was spending too much time on it, and wasn't doing anything inappropriate or embarrassing, but was just reading blogs, messaging her friends, and generally being distracted when she could be working on other, more important things. I noticed her habits too, and we both knew that the Bible speaks against unnecessary idleness in places like 1 Timothy 5:13, 1 Thessalonians 5:14, 2 Thessalonians 3:6, and multiple times in Proverbs. So we agreed to clear a spot upstairs in our bedroom where we could keep the computer, instead of at the desk in the living room. She knew that if it was upstairs she would be much less likely to just "hop on to check a few things" and then discover a lot more time has passed than she thought. It was a simple solution, but it helped her immensely, and not only did she get more done around the house, she felt good about the way she was spending her time.

One important thing we haven't talked about yet is that if you are going to help and guard your wife, then you need to be able to do it yourself. You cannot encourage your wife in her spiritual growth if you're not growing yourself. How can she take it seriously when her husband tells her to read her Bible, but rarely reads it himself? Or that she should be part of a small group when he's not? Or that she should look at her own struggles, when he doesn't look at his own? It certainly wouldn't last very long, and it would only create frustration on her part. Also, if you are growing and learning a lot for yourself, it will be much easier to guard her and guide her in what she does. When you're familiar with authors she might read, preachers she might listen to, or questions she might have, it stands to reason that you'll do a much better job of guarding her than if you just sent her on her way to figure it all out for herself.

It will also allow you to help her with any questions or problems she's wrestling with. When she doesn't understand something from her Bible reading or small group discussion or something like that, you should be able to explain it to her, or at least help her figure out the answer. That way you know she is getting good information that will be helpful for her. But again, you have to know it well yourself in order to give that good information, you can't fake it. That will probably just make things worse.

During a football game, the defensive back knows that it is his job to guard the end zone no matter what. He works hard to make sure that the attack of his opponent will not get through. The spiritual war that takes place around us is real and ongoing. Your wife and family are targets of attack. Take up your armor and guard them.

As Your Wife's Defensive Lineman... You Need to be Her Pursuer.

In 1982, the NFL introduced a new "official" stat. Whenever a defensive player tackled the opposing quarterback behind the line of scrimmage, he would be credited with a "sack." Thus began an era where certain defensive players were given a specific job: Get to the quarterback before he can throw the ball. Of course, it's not as simple as that, every player on the field has different responsibilities depending on the situation, the play call, the other players on the field, and other things, but there is a certain specialty to being a great pass-rusher. As soon as the ball is snapped, the defensive linemen, especially the ends, begin pursuing the quarterback relentlessly. They try to break through the blockers and get to the quarterback, never stopping until the ball is thrown or the play ends. They never stop pursuing. They never just stand there during the play doing nothing (and if they do, they find themselves without a job), and they never pursue any other player as long as the quarterback is still holding the ball. Men, as your wife's defensive lineman, you need to be her pursuer.

There is some question and controversy regarding the official league stats about sacks, because the league did not start counting them until 1982, but we can still pick out some of the best pursuers in league history. Bruce Smith played nineteen seasons for the Buffalo Bills and Washington Redskins as a Defensive End, and he is the only man in league history to have officially recorded 200 sacks. He would get past the blockers and pursue the quarterback with such intensity that he was able to play effectively until he was 40 years old, long past the normal age of NFL linemen. Of course, sacking the quarterback wasn't the only thing he did (he also recorded 1,078 tackles during his career), but it was his specialty. In his nineteen seasons, he got only two interceptions and defended only two passes. But he wasn't focused on things like that, he was concentrating on pursuing the quarterback. Another relentless pursuer in recent years is Jared Allen, who holds the official league record for most consecutive games with a sack with eleven. After only eight seasons, Allen has already recorded 105 sacks and has led the league twice, including with 22 sacks in 2011. When he joined the Minnesota Vikings, Allen said in his press conference that it was his job to get to the quarterback and he loved doing it.

The Defensive Lineman's pursuit of the quarterback is similar to how men pursue their potential wife, and that's a good thing. Proverbs 18:22 says, "He who finds a wife finds a good thing/ and obtains favor from the LORD." The unmarried men should notice that the proverb uses an active verb, "find." You're not going to find a great woman to marry by sitting at home watching sports, playing video games, and eating chips. You have to actually go out and find one. For a man to be lazy about finding a wife is not at all what the Lord intends, and we know this because He gives us multiple examples in the Bible of men (and their families) actively seeking a wife. One great example is the story of Isaac and Rebekah in Genesis 24. The story is actually more about Abraham and his servant than about Isaac, but the same principles apply. Abraham knew that Isaac would need a good wife, but they were living at the time among the Canaanites, and Abraham did not want Isaac to have a Canaanite wife. Instead, he wants Isaac to marry a woman from their own people. The same thing is true today. Christians need to marry Christians (2 Corinthians 6:14). So Abraham sent his servant to Nahor in Mesopotamia to find a wife for Isaac among their own people. The servant finds Rebekah and brings her back, which is when Isaac takes action. Knowing what his father wished and where Rebekah had come from, Isaac immediately takes her to be his wife. He doesn't ignore her, or say that they should get to know each other better, and he certainly doesn't ask her to live with him for a while so they can see if they would work out together (a philosophy unfortunately rampant in our current society). He knows that this woman would be a good wife, so he marries her.

Of course, our society sees marriage a little differently, and even I would admit that people probably shouldn't get married after meeting one time, but there is a lesson that applies from this story. Isaac and his father wanted him to get a good wife, so they pursued one. The pursuit of a potential wife now takes a couple of different forms. First, there is the pursuit of finding someone you may want to marry. This will likely need to involve meeting multiple people, going on dates, making decisions about who would or would not be a good wife, and probably even some disappointments. But eventually you will probably find a woman that you think would make a good wife, and you would like to marry her. The pursuit then becomes showing her that you are worth marrying. Pursuing her in this way shows her that you can take care of her, protect her, love her, challenge her, lead her, respect her, and that she will be happy being married to you for the rest of her life. This is what we like to call the dating phase. Make her feel special and show her that you would be a good, Godly husband.

For the married men, pursuing takes on a meaning that is similar, but different. Of course, a married man does not need to convince his wife to marry him. This is where a lot of guys fall short, including me. After the wedding, we tend to forget about pursuing our wives because we're married now, so that dating phase is over. But the dating phase isn't over, it's just changed now. Instead of showing her that you're going to be a good husband, show her that you'll *always* be a good husband. Show her that you will always love her and want to make her happy. Show her that she is important to you and always will be. By continuing to pursue her, you will create a feeling of enjoyment and fun in the marriage. How many times have you heard someone joke about how dating is so much fun, and it's too bad it leads to marriage? But it doesn't have to be that way. Marriage can be fun too, if you keep with the idea that you want to make her happy and enjoy being with you. Plan dates, trips, gifts, or anything else you think would be fun for her. Make her dinner, write her a poem, sing to her at karaoke night, or any of those silly things that seem so much fun when we're dating but tend to become extinct after the wedding.

One of the main skills of a great defensive lineman is the ability to change what he's doing to help his pursuit. If he keeps going one direction and that's not working, maybe he tries a different direction, or maybe he lines up in a slightly different spot, or maybe he tries a different move to get past the blocker. Whatever it is, he's aware when something isn't working and tries something new. The same idea applies to your wife. As the years go by, there will be many changes in your life. Circumstances, kids, preferences, living conditions, financial security, job changes, and any number of things will all change. But that doesn't stop the pursuit, it just changes it. Be aware of what's working and what's not. If your wife loved going to karaoke night when you were dating, but ten years later she doesn't like the atmosphere or music, find something else that she likes. If budget concerns won't allow a night to the theater, borrow a movie from a friend and have some popcorn at home. There's really no excuse for not finding some way to pursue your wife and show her that she's special. You just have to figure out how to do it.

There is one aspect of the defensive lineman's pursuit that we haven't talked much about yet, and that is the fact that he has to get past blockers. The offensive line tries to stop the pursuit, and the defensive lineman cannot do his job. The blocks we face in our current society and culture when pursuing our wives are not usually physical, but emotional and spiritual. Television shows, movies, magazines, and even casual conversations are constantly trying to show us that there is something better out there. A better standard of beauty, a better way to have fun, a better way people should treat you, and just a better way to live. And it's really easy to compare ourselves and our lives to other people and what they have, but that is a worthless exercise, and only serves to make us disappointed and frustrated. Funny, isn't it, how we only tend to compare ourselves to people who seem to be better off than we are, but never to the many people who are worse off than we are? Swimsuit magazines, television ads for products, self-help books, and other things like that are all trying to convince us that there is something better out there that we don't have. When you look at a provocative picture of a woman, you're telling your wife that she's not beautiful enough. When you don't make time for her, you're telling her that she's not important enough. When you speak to her disrespectfully or condescendingly, you're telling her that she's not smart enough. And that's exactly what Satan, through our culture, wants you both to think, because thinking that way can destroy a marriage and shatter the picture of Christ and His church that marriage is supposed to be.

Constantly pursuing your wife will help you avoid those blockers and stay focused on the woman that you committed to for the rest of your life. Figuring out what she may have fun doing, taking her on dates, spending time with her, and paying attention to how things may change will all help keep your focus on her and prevent you from getting blocked by so many things in this world. Solomon is a great example. Considered the wisest man who ever lived (outside of Jesus, of course), Solomon married a woman he was deeply in love with and they enjoyed each other immensely. Read the book Song of Solomon, and you'll see wonderful expressions of passionate love for each other. But then Solomon started getting sidetracked by the incredible riches he experienced. He took hundreds of wives and concubines, had more money than anyone could imagine, and filled his life with things of this world. The original passion that he had for his first wife was gone, cast aside by the allure of fame, riches, and women. But later in his life, Solomon realized the mistakes he had made and wrote the book of Ecclesiastes, where he realizes all the mistakes he has made and implores others not to do the same. This lesson may be best summed up by one sentence that Solomon wrote in Proverbs 5:15, "Drink water from your own cistern/ And fresh water from your own well." In other words, delight in what you have, and don't be tempted to go after other things in the hope that it will be better.

Which brings me to the most private, but possibly most important, aspect of pursuing your wife: Sex. It's not something that is talked about a lot, but I think it needs to be because it is such an important part of the marriage relationship. And let's not forget that sex is a wonderful gift from God, and we glorify Him when we enjoy it in the proper way. But sex has become a huge problem in our culture, and inside the church is no different. With so many ways to fall into sin, from movies and television to magazines and books to the internet and phone lines, it's no wonder that so many men and women fall victim to these traps. But what are we saying when we watch a certain movie, go to a certain website, or call a certain phone number? We're saying that we don't get what we need from our wives, either in frequency or quality, and that we need to get it from somewhere else. You may not be explicitly saying that to your wife, but that's what your actions are showing, and you're a fool if you think it doesn't affect the physical relationship you have with her.

So show your wife that she is the one you want to look at, touch, and make love to, nobody else, be they real or images. Initiate sex with her and make sure it's enjoyable for her. A lot of guys are afraid of wanting it too often so that their wives will get sick of it or wonder if there's something wrong with their husband. But trust me, if you do it right, I don't think any woman will get tired of it, and it's way better for a woman to think that her husband finds her so attractive, so sexy, and so appealing that he can't help but want to make love to her every day than it is for a woman to believe that her husband finds her unappealing and is uninterested in her. But the same basic keys to pursuing are still in effect. Figure out what she likes, what will make it good for her, and make sure she knows that you're not just interested in meeting your own desires, but in expressing a love to her that you can't do any other way.

There can be a lot that goes into making sure that sex is enjoyable for your wife. First, understand that men and women are different. What works for men usually does not work for women. A man can be ready for sex in the blink of an eye, but with most women the process is much longer. That's not to say there's no spontaneity, but rather that it is easier to have great sex if preparing your wife for it becomes how you live, not just a means to an end. One thing to remember is that women are not usually visually stimulated like men are. While the vast majority of men are turned on by scantily-clad models and plunging necklines, only a small percentage of women like looking at men that way. So becoming the stereotypical "hunk" with bulging muscles and perfect hair may not be, and probably isn't, what your wife is looking for. But that doesn't mean she isn't affected by your appearance. Why would she want to be intimate with someone who is dirty, smells, and dresses like a slob? Be aware of what she likes and go with it. Does she like it when you dress a certain way, wear your hair a certain way, or smell a certain way? Then do it. Maybe it's how often you shave (or don't), or how often you cut your toenails, or when you shower that makes her sit up and take notice. But whatever it is, do it the way she likes it, and your physical relationship will thrive.

Some men don't like that type of thinking because it means they don't always get to do things their way. After all, it's our own body, right? We should get to do with it what we want! Actually, no, if you claim to be a Christian, your body does not belong to you. Paul wrote about both ideas in 1 Corinthians when he says in chapter six, "The body is not meant for sexual immorality, but for the Lord, and the Lord for the body...Do you not know that your bodies are members of Christ?" (vs. 13, 15) and then in chapter seven, "For the wife does not have authority over her own body, but the husband does. Likewise the husband does not have authority over his own body, but the wife does" (v. 4). As you can see, your body is not your own. First, it belongs to the Lord, and second, it belongs to your wife. This also goes back to the idea from Ephesians 5 that husbands should sacrifice for their wives and do anything possible to love them and make them happy.

But it's not just your looks or cleanliness that makes you attractive to your wife. Like I said before, few women are stimulated in visual ways like men are. So you may have to be a bit creative and discover what it is that your wife likes. Leaving her love notes, bringing her flowers, lighting candles, or even just complimenting her are all examples of things that may get your wife "in the mood." And often it doesn't have to be anything elaborate or mushy. One of the things my wife likes best is when I call her from work to see how her day is going. It's a quick, simple thing, but it makes her feel like I'm thinking about her and connected to our family even when I'm away. That small act makes us both feel like we care about each other and are connected to each other, which translates to better intimacy. And when you make it a way of living instead of just doing it one day hoping to get lucky, she'll know that you really care and want those feelings to carry through the whole marriage, not just one night.

Unmarried men, don't think this last section doesn't apply to you yet; It absolutely does. Everything you do now will affect your future marriage, and I don't just mean physically, I mean everything, but sex is what we're focusing on right now. When you look at a website, watch a movie, or call a phone number, you're still making a statement to your wife, even though you may not know her yet. You're telling her that she's not special enough to wait for, and that you don't think it will be good enough with her when you get married so you're going to find something better right now. But being able to one day tell your new wife, "This is what I've been waiting for, and I've never done this with anyone else" is an amazing feeling, and shows that you've been loving her for years, even without knowing her. The difficulties, joys, questions, lessons, and wonders of sex do not start on the wedding night. They start years before you even know your wife's name. And don't think just about your own wife, but everyone else's. When you date someone, it's possible that you are dating someone else's eventual wife. As men, we are called to protect the purity not just of our wives, but of all women. We want to do what we can to help others honor the

Lord, and that involves not causing each other to stumble. By treating all women with respect and love, we can help each other act in a way that glorifies God. The women we have relationships with before we're married can tell their husband someday that they have not given themselves to any other man.

Defensive Linemen don't try to pursue the quarterback sometimes, they do it all the time. And they don't pursue half-heartedly, but with passion and intensity. Be your wife's pursuer, men. Don't be content to pursue her until you're married, but keep pursuing her for the rest of your life. Don't get blocked by things in this world, but fight past them. Do it passionately and joyfully, and show her that she is what you want, and nothing else.

12

As Your Wife's Referee...
You Need to be Her Whistle Blower.

It has been said that sports are simple. Break it down to the smallest level, and there's almost nothing to it. Basketball? Put the ball in the hoop. Hockey? Put the puck in the net. Baseball? Hit the ball with a bat and run in a big circle. Football? Run across a line holding a ball without falling down. That doesn't seem hard at all. But then you add in the about 400 rules of the game in the NFL rule book, and suddenly it doesn't seem very easy. There are a lot of things to remember, but that shouldn't matter, should it? Everyone playing in the game will take it upon themselves to make sure they are following each rule and playing the game how they are supposed to, self-policing the rules so there are no arguments, controversies, or misunderstandings, right? Well, in a perfect world, that's how it would be. But we don't live in a perfect world, we live in a fallen world. Offensive lineman don't call themselves for holding, running backs don't spot the ball themselves, defensive backs don't out themselves for interference, and nobody will penalize themselves for hitting after the whistle or out of bounds. This is why every sport needs officials. Referees, judges, linesman, and umpires are all there to make sure that the rules are followed and the game is being played properly. If somebody breaks the rules, the official blows his whistle and makes the call. It's imperative to the game to have someone in a position of authority making sure that everyone is playing how they should play and following the rules. Men, as your wife's referee, you need to be her whistle blower.

The immediate impact of not breaking the rules is obvious. When you do something you're not supposed to do, you are moved farther away from your goal. Sometimes just five yards, sometimes up to 15 yards, but in any case the fact remains that it is now more difficult to score. If you play the way you're supposed to, reaching your goal and winning will be easier.

The same concept applies to our lives. When we live the way the Lord has called us to live and follow the truths that are given in His Word, we move closer to the ultimate goal of glorifying Him and showing His love. When we don't, we move away from Him and His truths and it becomes much more difficult to reach the goal that He has given us. But like a player in a football game, will we police ourselves? Will we call ourselves out when we commit a penalty? Sometimes, maybe, but certainly not all the time. Sometimes we don't realize we committed a penalty because we didn't know the rules well enough. Sometimes it was just a total accident. Or sometimes we just give in to our sinful habits and hit that quarterback helmet-first after the whistle. In any of those cases, we may admit we did wrong and seek forgiveness, but many times we may not. That's why we need to help each other live the way we should. All authority is God's, but he gives us friends and family and relationships so that we can help each other in this life. Proverbs 27:17 says, "Iron sharpens iron, and one man sharpens another." We need to help each other honor the Lord in our lives, and the most important person we can help do that is our wives.

The first important thing to remember is that correction should never be done for our own purposes. We don't correct people to make things easier on ourselves or because we want to get them back for something they said to us or even because it would make the house run more smoothly or anything like that. We correct people so that they can honor the Lord with how they are living, acting, and speaking, like James 5:19-20 says, "My brothers, if anyone among you wanders from the truth and someone brings him back, let him know that whoever brings back a sinner from his wandering will save his soul from death and will cover a multitude of sins." See the point of correction? To save people's souls, not to make life easier for ourselves. We need to focus everything on God above ourselves. If the reason you are correcting someone is for your own personal gain, you need to stop and take a look at your own heart and decide how you can best honor God yourself.

Another important thing that needs to be said about this topic is that we are not talking about being judgemental. We are all sinners, and we all fall short of the way we should live (Romans 3:23). We are talking about helping, correcting, and teaching. It should never be done in anger or frustration, but rather with a focus on helping the person understand how God wants them to live. Paul makes this point in a few of his letters. 2 Timothy 2:24-26 says, "And the Lord's servant must not be quarrelsome but kind to everyone, able to teach, patiently enduring evil, correcting his opponents with gentleness. God may perhaps grant them repentance leading to a knowledge of the truth, and they may come to their senses and escape from the snare of the devil, after being captured by him to do his will." There again we see that the point of being gentle and correcting is to point them to

God. Ephesians 4:29 says, "Let no corrupting talk come out of your mouths, but only such as is good for building up, as fits the occasion, that it may give grace to those who hear." That verse can be applied to a lot of situations and emotions, but it definitely applies to correcting someone. And in Galatians it says, "Brothers, if anyone is caught in any transgression, you who are spiritual should restore him in a spirit of gentleness. Keep watch on yourself, lest you too be tempted" (6:1). That verse is particularly interesting because not only does it tell us to be gentle, but warns us to watch out for ourselves too. Getting angry and frustrated and bitter at somebody for doing something you don't like is sinful, so if that's how we approach them, not only are we not helping them, we're falling into sin ourselves.

One of the most important ways to make sure that you are correcting someone gently and with a good heart is to do it according to the rules of the authority. A referee doesn't get to make up his own rules before the game starts or even as the game goes on. The teams wouldn't know what was expected of them, coaches and players would get confused and angry, and eventually the game would just fall apart. That's why the NFL gives everyone the official rulebook. When everyone is looking at the same source, it takes away confusion and makes sure that all the expectations are clear. It also serves as the final authority. If there's a disagreement about the rules, everyone can go to the rulebook and see what it says.

Now, the Bible is not just a rule book. Make no mistake, it does give us rules, laws, and commands that tell us how to live or not live. But it's much more than a rule book. It tells us all of those things so that we can glorify God and love Him and be in relationship with Him. And it is our final authority. Everything we do, say, and think should be tested against the Bible to see if it holds up. Of course, the Bible being the ultimate authority is an idea that a lot of people don't believe, but all Christians' lives should be based on 2 Timothy 3:14-17. If we are going to live our lives a certain way, we need an authority to follow that tells us how to live. It cannot just be ourselves and our own conscience, it cannot be the culture we live in, and it cannot be different for each person so it "fits." All of those things have problems and will fail. But the Bible does not fail. It is the Word of God and the ultimate truth. I'm not going to keep harping on this because it's a large idea and entire books have been written on the topic. So if you want to learn more about the authority of the Bible, dive into that topic with books, sermons, and pastors and you will learn a lot. I'll just leave it here with the point that the Bible is true, without error, and the ultimate authority that we have (2 Timothy 3:16).

With that said, what do you need to do in order to correct your wife according to the Bible? Simply put, you need to know what the Bible says. How can you correct anyone according to God's Word if you don't know what God's Word is talking about? When a coach questions a referee's call, does the referee respond by saying, "Well, I think that's the rule, but I haven't actually read the rule book, so I'm kind of guessing"? Even though a lot of us may believe that the officials have not read the rule book during our team's game, they actually put in a ton of time studying, questioning, and practicing the book to make sure that they guide everyone's actions correctly. This goes back to the first chapter on being your wife's scout. You have to study the Bible in order to know what it says, and then you'll be able to guide her and help her live the way the Bible calls her to live. The other thing you need to be doing is living God's way yourself and be open to correction yourself. It's much easier to take correction from someone who is willing to accept it and change what they're doing than from someone who doles out advice but refuses to change their own behaviors. That's also why it's so important to use the Bible as your guide and your reason when correcting your wife. If you can discuss the issue with her and show her the Biblical reasons that a change is needed, she will understand that it is not just your own desire or selfishness that is bringing on the discussion, it's because you love her and want her to honor the Lord. She'll also know that you're not correcting her to meet your standards, but God's standards.

That's an important thing that you need to able to recognize. What is the difference between the way that we want things and the way that God wants things? It's not easy, because a lot of the things that we want are the same as what God wants, but our motivation is very different. I want my wife to love and respect me, but do I want that because God wants it or because it will make me feel superior and she'll do what I tell her to? See, that's the key. What is your motivation? If your motivation is selfish, that is sinful, but if your motivation is centered on Christ, He will help you guide and teach your wife so that you can both honor Him.

Another difference you'll need to be able to recognize is things that are sinful vs. things that are bothersome. Putting the toilet paper on the holder so that it rolls from the back, while ridiculous and absurd, is not sinful. Nowhere in the Bible does God tell us how to put our toilet paper (probably because He figured any sane person would put it the correct way, from the front). So if my wife puts it the wrong way, I might tell her, "I know this isn't a huge deal, but it just really bothers me when the toilet paper rolls from the back, would you mind putting it the other way?" If she insists it should go on backwards, I may just let it go, because it's not a sin issue, it's just something I like a certain way. However, it can become a sin issue if she mocks me for caring about that or refuses to change it out of spite or something like that. In that case, the toilet paper issue becomes secondary. Now we need to deal with sin issues of respect, submission, and attitude, all of which I can go to the Bible and explain to her why it is important to God that she acts a certain way towards her husband. I don't even necessarily care about the toilet paper anymore, I care about my wife's heart and her relationship with Christ. But again, it can be difficult sometimes to figure out what is or isn't a sin issue, and what you should do about it or how you should approach it, and this where help from other officials can really come into play.

Just like a referee has a whole team of officials to make sure everyone is sticking to the rules, you also need to have other guys that you can go to with questions or concerns about what your wife is doing, how you should respond, and if the concern is even Biblically relevant. Having those other guys around for advice will help you respond appropriately and not get yourself into tough situations when you either didn't respond to your wife when you should have, or responded too harshly when you didn't need to. Mistakes can often be avoided just by seeking good council and getting some other perspectives before making a decision.

Of course, the big question is, "How is she going to respond?" This is what stops most people from correcting others, and especially people who are close to us. We don't want anger, hurt feelings, awkwardness or bitterness, so maybe we'll just let that thing go and then we don't have to deal with it. But that is simply a recipe for disaster down the road. If you don't face a problem now, it will become an even bigger problem in the future. But how will your wife respond when you do? It's entirely possible that she will respond with humility, respect, and repentance, and the issue will be solved. If that happens, praise the Lord for her willing heart! But, it's also possible that she does not respond like that. One of the most common responses by anyone who is being corrected is to get defensive and turn it back on the other person. Your wife may tell you that it's your fault and that if you would do something differently she wouldn't have to do that. Or she may say that you sin too so why are you talking to her about her sin? The best way to avoid a reaction like that is to not give her an opportunity to have it. Do what you need to do, treat her respectfully, make sure her needs are being met, and if you do that she won't be able to accuse you of being a hypocrite. More importantly, turn to the Bible and show her that everyone's sin is their own responsibility. You can of course apologize and repent of your sin as well, but it certainly doesn't excuse her sinful behavior at all.

Your wife may also respond by questioning your understanding of what the Bible is saying about the issue. If that happens, dive into it together. What does the Bible say? How is it to be understood? This will not only guide you both toward the answer revealed in the Bible, but it will make you grow closer as a couple in your relationship with the Lord, and hopefully you will both come to a deeper understanding of the Biblical issue.

It is also possible that your wife will refuse to listen to you and make no effort to understand or change. If the problem at hand is an issue of sin that she will not stop, continue praying for her and trying to talk to her about the issue using the Bible, not your own emotion. If that doesn't work, it may be time to meet with a pastor or elder so they can support what you're saying and help her understand how she is sinning and what to do about it. It may take a long time, a lot of hard conversations, and a lot of prayer, but it will be worth it if she turns from her sin to be the wife that God wants her to be.

Look at the verse from James 5:19-20 again: "My brothers, if anyone among you wanders from the truth and someone brings him back, let him know that whoever brings back a sinner from his wandering will save his soul from death and will cover a multitude of sins." Men, the greatest thing you can do for your wife is to help her honor the Lord

Jesus Christ and live for His glory. Do not turn a blind eye when she is wandering. Throw the yellow flag and help her get back on the right path. It may be uncomfortable and difficult, but you may be saving her soul from death.

Epilogue

The Draft

After every season, all 32 teams come together for an event that has become a huge spectacle: The NFL Draft. Sportswriters try to guess whom each team will pick, whole websites and magazines are devoted to the process, and the teams themselves spend a ton of time, energy, and money, all for an event that lasts a few days and then is gone until the next year. Why is so much invested in this? Why such incredible attention for the draft? Simply because the teams know that it is their main chance to improve.

On May 19, 1935, the nine NFL owners approved a plan that would allow the worst teams in the league to get better. After the following season, the teams held the first NFL draft, with the Philadelphia Eagles making the first ever pick, drafting Jay Berwanger out of the University of Chicago. Like we talked about in the first chapter, scouting of college players at that time was nothing near what it is now, but the draft still provided the weakest teams the opportunity to improve. As technology and football philosophies have advanced, so has teams' chances of improving themselves through the draft. For one of the best examples, we'll go back to the Indianapolis Colts. In 1997 the Colts went 3-13, and received the first pick in the next year's draft. They used that pick to select Peyton Manning, who went through some growing pains as the Colts finished 3-13 again in 1998, and then used the 4th overall pick in the draft to select Edgerrin James, who over the next few years would be one of the best running backs in the league. In 1999, the Colts finished 13-3 and won their division. Over the next 13 seasons, with Manning leading the way the whole time, the Colts won their division eight times and played in two Super Bowls, winning it in 2006. When the Colts lost Manning to a neck injury before the 2011 season, they finished 2-14 and once again drafted a quarterback with the first overall pick, Andrew Luck out of Stanford, who was considered one of the best quarterback prospects in recent years. With Luck under center in 2012, the Colts finished 11-5 and again made the playoffs.

It may seem like an easy decision for the Colts. If you have a terrible year because your quarterbacks are not very good, draft a different quarterback to make your team better. But a lot of thought and study goes into the question of whom each team should draft. Every team identifies their strengths and weaknesses and enters the draft accordingly. No team is going to draft a player if they already have a lot of great players at that position. They decide which positions on their team need the most work, and then they pick the players they think will help them improve.

The same idea applies to us as husbands. Everyone is good at some things and not as good at others, and as you read through this book you probably came across some positions that you feel good about in your own marriage and other positions that could use a lot of work. Thankfully, you have a chance to improve yourself in all of those positions.

The first thing you need to do, of course, is to figure out how you're doing at each position. If you are a great running back, be encouraged by that and keep working to stay strong at that position (after all, even Walter Payton still worked with coaches and kept trying to get better). If you're not a very good defensive lineman, start working on trying to improve in that way. But there are a lot of positions, and a lot of us struggle with more than one, and sometimes even several, so where do we start? First, don't discount your own feelings. If you feel like you're good at something, embrace that, and if you feel like you're bad at something, accept that. Much of the time, people have a good sense of their own abilities. But it's always good to have another opinion, so where else can you go? To the person most affected by you: Your wife. She will be able to tell you in what areas she feels you're strong and which ones need improvement. Like I said earlier in the book, I had my wife score me 1-10 on every position, and that gave me a great idea of where I needed to improve. It also showed me the difference between how I thought I was doing and how she thought I was doing. Some positions I thought I was really good at, she agreed, but on other positions I had a high opinion of myself while she felt it was lacking. It really helped to talk with her about it and hear what she needed most from me and where I needed to improve to help our marriage.

My recommendation is to examine yourself first and figure out what you're good at and what you need to improve. Try a scoring system, or maybe "Good, Medium, Bad" columns, or whatever it is that helps you identify strengths and weaknesses. Then have your wife do the same thing for you. That will open up discussion about what both of you think about the marriage and what both of you need from your spouse. Next, look at the positions that need the most attention and decide how much priority should be given to each one. There's no magic ranking that says how important each position is (though most people would agree that some are more important), it's mostly a matter of what your wife needs and how much improvement needs to happen. When my wife scored me on each position, the lowest scores she gave me were on quarterback and wide receiver while the highest were on head coach and running back. Looking at the two positions I needed to improve on the most, we decided that quarterback was the most important and the most vital to being a Godly husband. We then talked about what I could do to improve as the leader of our family. A lot of really good, practical ideas came out of that discussion, and over the next couple of years I got a lot better at it. I also thought about wide receiver and what I could do to improve in that area, so for our next anniversary I planned activities for a whole weekend while our kids stayed with my mom. Now, when special occasions come up, I remember that being a good wide receiver is important to her and makes her feel special.

Of course, one of the great things about the draft is that it happens after every season. If a team picks a player to improve at a position and he doesn't work out, they can pick another player at that position the next year. And if you try something to improve yourself at a position for your wife and it doesn't work, you can try something else. A team doesn't have to keep a player forever if he's not playing well, and you don't have to keep doing the same thing if it's not helping. Try to figure out what went wrong and then try to improve in some other way.

But sometimes a team picks a great player who turns out to be a Hall of Famer for their team. That's awesome when it happens, but is that player going to be on the team forever? Of course not, eventually that player will get older and not quite as good, or maybe he'll sign with a new team or retire, and the team will have to improve that position again. The player may have helped for a while, even a long while, but eventually the team will need to draft somebody new for that position. You may figure out how to improve a position of yours and it may work really well for a while, but eventually it may not work anymore and you'll have to try something new. You can't be satisfied with making one change one time, you have to be constantly aware of how you're doing and always looking at ways that you can possibly improve, even if you're already doing a good job. That's what will keep you in tune with the marriage and focused on your wife, which will in turn help both of you stay focused on Christ and the calling He has for both of you.

And that's really the whole goal of the entire exercise, isn't it? To glorify God and spread the gospel, and the most important person you can do that with is your wife. It doesn't end there, obviously, but it starts there. 1 Timothy 3:5 says, "for if someone does not know how to manage his own household, how will he care for God's church?" The verses in that section are specifically talking about leaders in the church, but every man can take them to heart knowing that all of his relationships, attitudes, and opinions begin in the home, and especially with his wife. Care for her, love her, cherish her, and most of all, glorify God with her. You may not be elected to any sort of Hall of Fame, but you will be able to celebrate with Jesus for eternity.